A Practical Step-by-Step Guide to

CREATIVE
GARDEN
IDEAS

A Practical Step-by-Step Guide to

CREATIVE GARDEN IDEAS

WHITECAP BOOKS

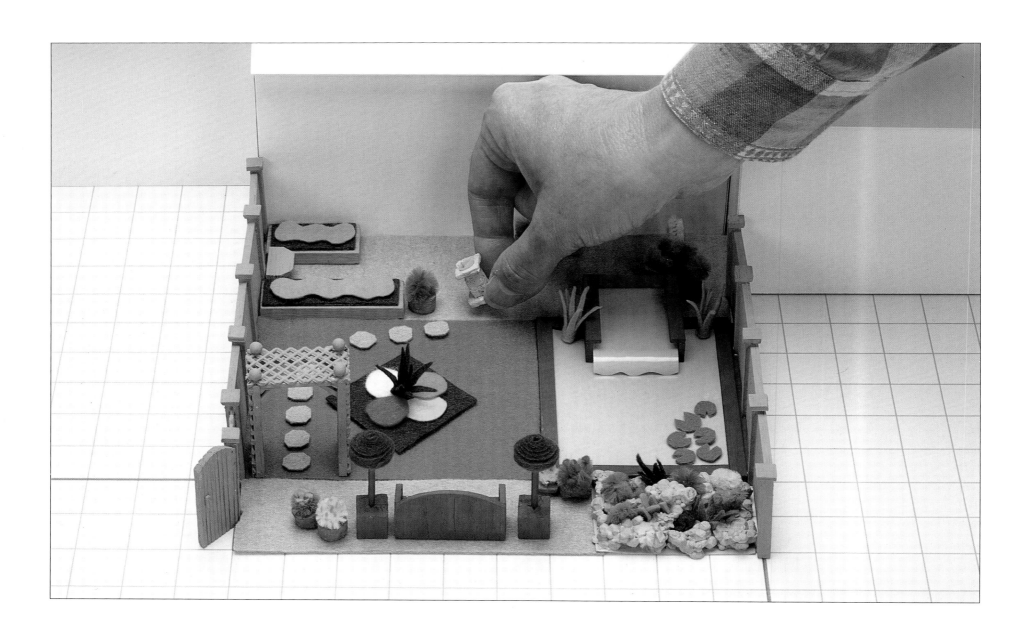

4142
This edition published in 1997 by Whitecap Books Ltd.,
351 Lynn Avenue North Vancouver, B.C., Canada V7J 2C4
© 1997 CLB International, Godalming, Surrey, England
All rights reserved.

Printed in Singapore
ISBN 1-55110-500-4

Credits

Edited and designed: Ideas into Print
Step-by-step photographs: Neil Sutherland
Typesetting: Ideas into Print and Ash Setting and Printing
Production Director: Gerald Hughes
Production: Ruth Arthur, Neil Randles, Paul Randles,
Janine Seddon, Karen Staff

Half-title page: Wooden decking makes a natural background for many plants. Here it is successfully teamed with conifers and hostas.
Opposite title page: A miniature pool, complete with bell fountain, in a wooden barrel makes a delightful water feature for the small garden.
Title page: Plunging pots into a windowbox makes it easy to replace individual plants and keep the display looking its best.
Left: Planning your garden with the aid of scale models for all the major features gives you an excellent impression of the finished result.
Right: Given good drainage and enough water, a potted rock garden will thrive in a sunny spot. A well-filled container looks mature straightaway.

CONTENTS
PLANS AND PATIOS

Below: Siting trees correctly is a crucial element of garden planning.

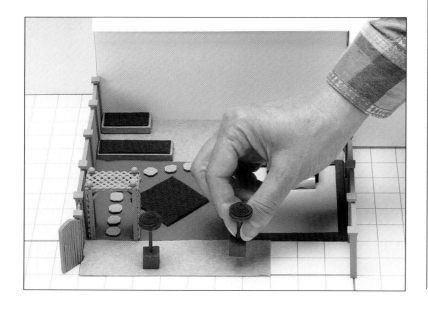

Above: Consider the design possibilities of foliage shapes and colors.

Above: Summer-flowering annuals in a wall basket make a fine show.

Below: Liven up an expanse of patio with a colorful bedding scheme.

CONTENTS
WATER AND CONTAINERS

Below: A fountain is easy to install and adds interest to a garden pond.

Above: Water lilies vary in size and spread; choose them with care.

Above: A traditional hanging basket can be enjoyed all summer long.

Below: Look for well-shaped, good-quality plants to fill containers.

Part One

PLANNING YOUR GARDEN

You can create a beautiful and successful garden without employing an expensive landscape architect - the key is good planning. By following a few practical pointers and adding a little personal flair and imagination, good planning can transform your raw new plot, untamed jungle or cramped and gloomy backyard into your dream garden in a single season. The first step is to get to know exactly what you have: the size, shape and orientation of the site, plus any existing major features. The aim is then to emphasize the best points and hide or disguise the bad ones. But before you even start to consider the practicalities of this, it is important that you have a clear idea of the style of garden and the kind of features you are keen to include in the final plan. This will make decisions much easier during the planning stage and produce a finished garden with cohesion and balance. The first part of this book takes you easily and logically through the stages of planning a garden. The ideas here are only suggestions; it is much more important that you have fun with your own.

Left: A weeping pear tree at the focal point of a formal garden.   *Above:* Hostas are superb architectural plants.

First thoughts

So where do you start? Before you rush out and start digging and planting, take a tip from the professionals and experiment on paper first. Begin by sizing up the site. Measure around the perimeter and draw up a plan to scale on graph paper. Now you can see what you have to work with, you can mark in any existing features and indicate the particularly sunny or shady areas. This is important when choosing certain plants and features. Now before you go any further, draw up a list of all the elements you would like to see included in your ideal garden: maybe a fine lawn, a patio area, traditional flower beds, an ornamental pool, and so on. There might not be room for all of them - although most features can be scaled down to suit - but this will help you shortlist those you consider the most important. You can get clever ideas to stimulate your imagination from all kinds of sources: photographs in books, television gardening programs, annual shows and exhibitions or local gardens open to the public. At this point you can have fun making scale models of your new garden features to give you a real impression of how it is going to look. Or you could use toy modelling bricks or cut pictures from gardening catalogs and magazines to simulate the effect you are aiming for. It is worth spending a few hours at your local garden center, not only to absorb garden ideas, but also to see what features and materials are readily available. Now is also a good time to take note of the cost, as this may affect your plans. Even a small item might inspire you and trigger off an idea for a feature or a total look for the garden. If you can develop a theme for the whole garden, or even a part of it, you will achieve a far more balanced and professional looking result with everything, even the plants, chosen to fit in.

Making models

The models featured in the first part of this book are easy to create from simple materials such as paper, card, felt and balsa wood. The trellis panels are cut from sheets of perforated plastic made for tapestry. The ornamental spheres on the top of fence posts and arches are simply painted map pins. The illusion of water is easy to achieve by sticking clear adhesive plastic over blue paper. Model shops can supply a wide range of paints - the ones that dry to a matt finish are best - and other materials that you can use to make attractive and useful models.

The model houses are purposely neutral in color and style to avoid drawing attention away from the garden design. In the real world, the size, style and position of houses have a great influence over the gardens they overlook.

It is vital to build up your model on a piece of paper or card marked with squares and to use the same scale for all the features in the garden. The scale for the models in this book is based on each of these squares representing one square meter (just over 3ft x3ft) in the real world.

Although they take a little longer to put together, it is worth making three-dimensional models of trees to gain a real impression of how they look when mature. It is also useful to shine a spotlight from one side to simulate where the shade falls.

Cut out pieces of felt for the flat features in the garden, such as lawns, paths, patios and beds. Make several different shapes for each and mix and match them until you like the result. Designing a garden can be fun!

Choosing your boundaries

The boundaries of the garden plot should be your first consideration when planning the total look and style of your hoped-for scheme. They are easily overlooked in the excitement of planning a garden, but what goes on around the perimeter is not as unobtrusive and irrelevant as you might think; in fact it can have a considerable influence on the final effect and should be designed in conjunction with other major features. Most likely, you will have inherited some kind of wall, fence or trellis, which may or may not be suitable. Replacement can be expensive, so you might have to compromise by redesigning certain areas at first, say around key spaces such as the patio. If you find the effect totally unacceptable, resort to some kind of disguise or cover-up, such as inexpensive trellis, climbing plants or decorative screens. First decide whether the structure is doing the job for which it is intended; a lightweight post and rail fence is fine where you want to appreciate a fine view beyond the garden, but for privacy or shelter you need something more substantial. Before constructing or changing any permanent structure, check exactly which boundaries you or your neighbor are responsible for and make sure there are no local planning restrictions on size and style.

Below: Timber fence posts and panels are available in various styles. Allow the timber to weather, or stain or paint it to suit your scheme.

Boundary walls

A wall is more expensive and time-consuming to build, but it is maintenance-free, durable and offers better security for vulnerable gardens. Old, second-hand bricks produce an instantly mellow effect, but new bricks come in many colors and shades for creating interesting patterns. Alternatively, cover the wall with climbing plants fixed to special hooks and wires or trained over a detachable trellis. An old and dominant existing wall often benefits from being painted white to add a little light.

Below: A hedge takes longer to establish, but makes an attractive, natural background for other features.

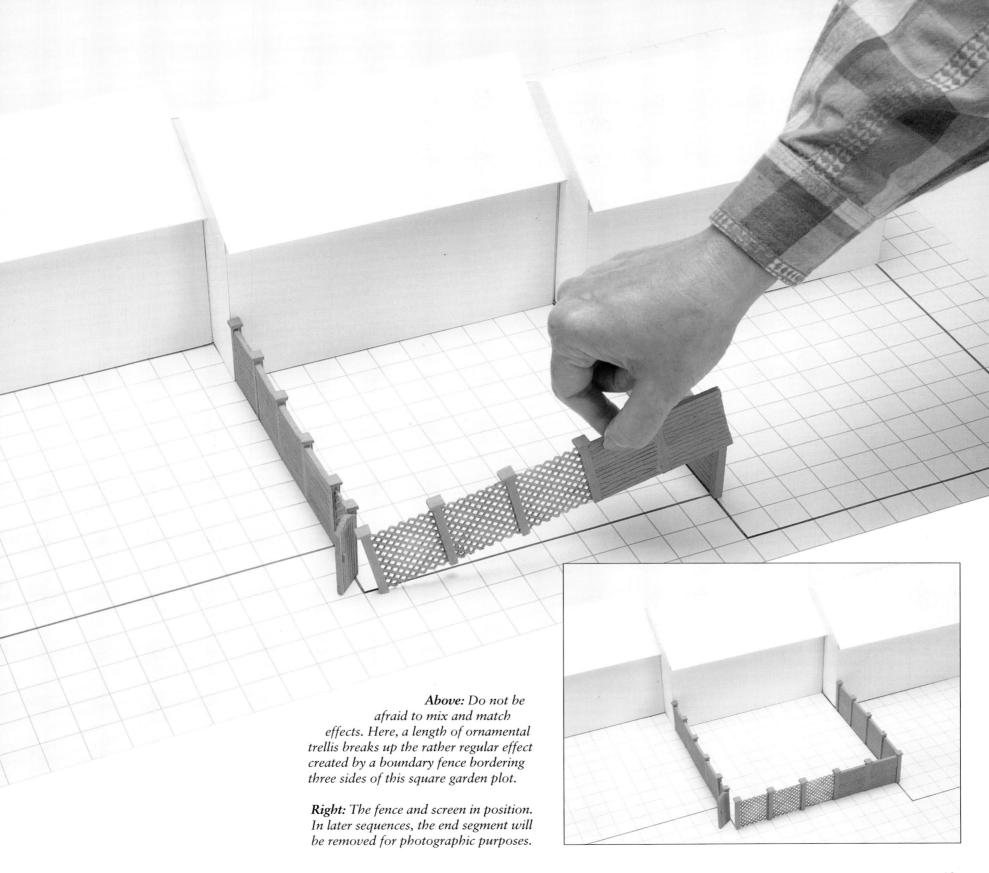

Above: *Do not be afraid to mix and match effects. Here, a length of ornamental trellis breaks up the rather regular effect created by a boundary fence bordering three sides of this square garden plot.*

Right: *The fence and screen in position. In later sequences, the end segment will be removed for photographic purposes.*

Left: Sometimes it is better to site the patio at the further end of the garden, if this is where it will receive most sunshine.

Siting the patio

The patio is essentially an outdoor living area, a firm, dry level surface where you can relax in the sunshine or enjoy an alfresco meal. Although the most convenient place for a patio is close to the house, try and site it where it will receive maximum sunshine. This may mean a spot at the opposite end of the garden, in which case provide some form of permanent dry access from the house, such as a path or stepping stones. The size and shape of your patio can be an important element in the overall impact and success of your garden. If the traditional square or rectangle looks too formal or does little for a small, regular plot, experiment with curves and circles. Break up areas of hard landscaping with a change of level or integrated features, such as raised beds, a patio pool, built-in furniture or even a barbecue. Sometimes the choice of paving materials will influence the final shape and size of the area, so it makes sense to have some idea of how you want the patio to look before you make your final decision. If you can calculate the area using complete bricks, blocks or pavers, you will save yourself a lot of cutting and fitting at construction stage, as well as expensive wastage of materials.

Introducing a curve and a slight change of level is instantly softer and changes the whole look of the garden. Use your imagination at the early planning stages.

A free-standing patio makes an interesting option providing it can be well sheltered. Here, a circle is a good choice to liven up a regular square plot.

Positioning patios for the sun

Observe your garden during the course of the day to establish which areas are the sunniest at certain times. You could plan for two or even more patio areas, each serving a different purpose or designed to catch the best of the sun at different times of the day.

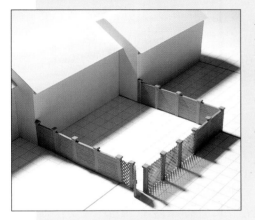

Left: Here, the house shades the area immediately beyond the back door for most of the day. This spot is unlikely to make a successful patio.

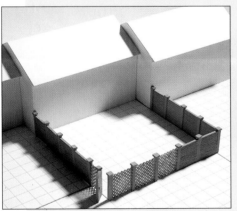

Left: An adjoining or nearby building may cast unwelcome shadows on certain parts of the garden.

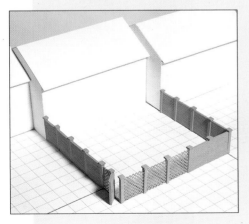

Left: In this situation, the whole garden is enjoying the benefits of full sunshine and only the front of the building is in shade.

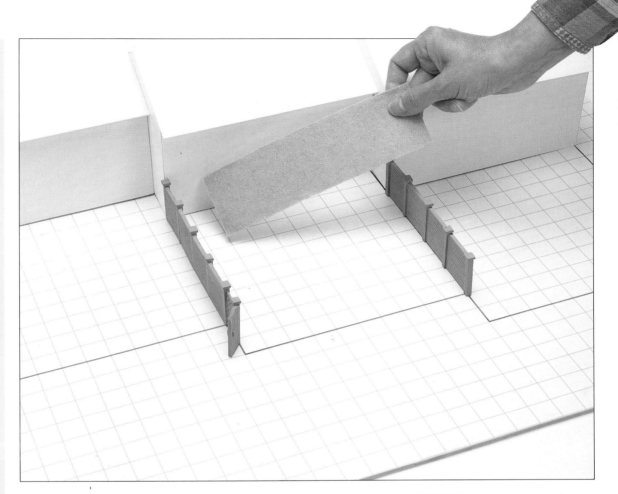

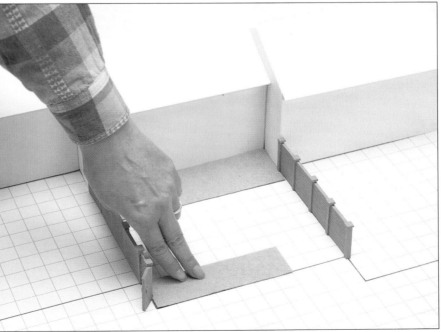

1 In the garden design shown above, the main patio is situated immediately behind the house, as this is the area that receives maximum sunshine right through the day.

2 A smaller paved seating area at the opposite end of the garden makes an excellent additional feature visually and is designed to catch the last rays of the afternoon sun.

Choosing the shape of your lawn

Grassy areas are not simply there to fill in the gaps between other features. A well-planned lawn can be an excellent design feature, even a focal point, if its shape and size is thoughtfully integrated into your general garden plan. Although a lawn requires a certain level of commitment in terms of maintenance, with trimming, watering, feeding and aerating during the growing season, grass is quick and easy to establish - whether from seed or turves - and can be adapted to any size or shape. However formal, it can offer a wonderfully soft, very natural effect that you could never achieve with an expanse of paving or hard landscaping and is complementary to all other features and materials. A lawn, especially where it has been planted in a definitive geometric shape such as a circle, rectangle or square, makes an excellent setting or surround for other features, such as a pond, a statue, flower beds or a sundial.

Above: A circular lawn immediately softens the hard-edged boundaries of a square plot and creates a more informal feel to the garden.

Above: Instead of positioning a square lawn dead center of a square site, try placing it on the diagonal, which produces a far more interesting effect.

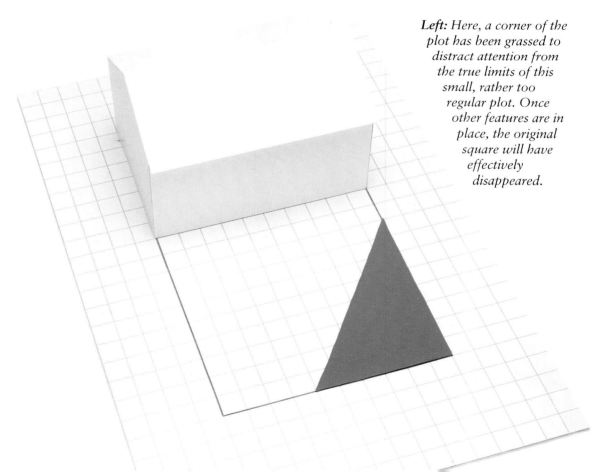

Left: Here, a corner of the plot has been grassed to distract attention from the true limits of this small, rather too regular plot. Once other features are in place, the original square will have effectively disappeared.

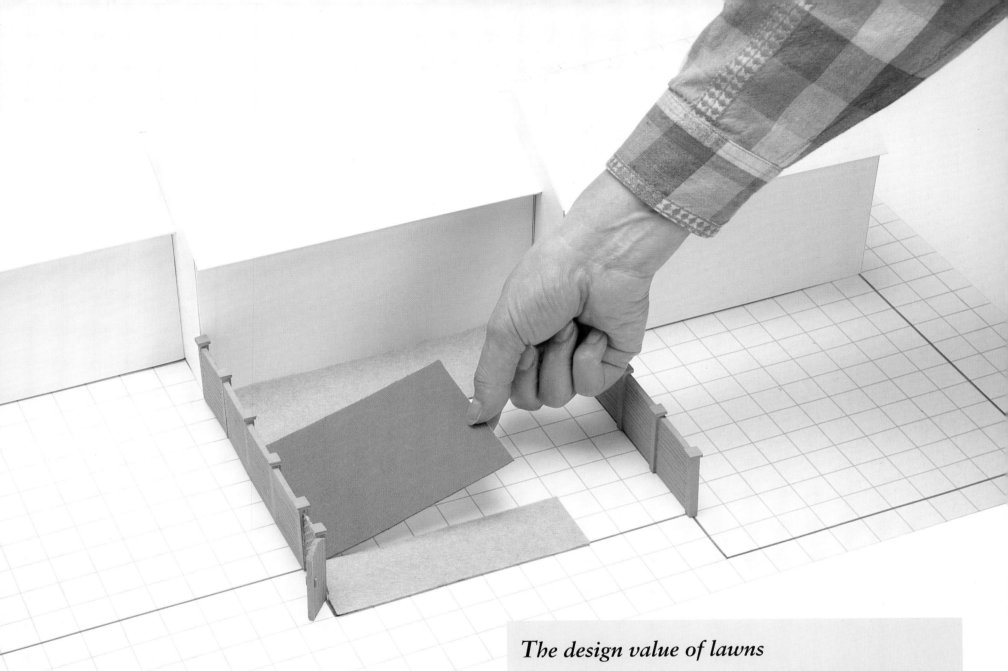

Above: Here, a rectangular lawn forms part of the emerging design for this garden. Experiment with different shapes and sizes of lawn in conjunction with other features until you find something that looks good from every angle.

The design value of lawns

You can use the lawn to link larger features, or to influence the visual impact of your garden as a whole. Its length, width, shape and position can make the plot appear wider, larger or simply more interesting than it actually is. Remember to plan an area of grass from a practical point of view, so that it is relatively easy to maintain. All parts must be accessible to your mower, with no areas narrower than the width of the machine. When experimenting with shapes, bear in mind that curves and circles create a softer, informal look, while harder, geometric figures, such as squares and rectangles, appear more formal. Try positioning your shapes on the diagonal or slightly at an angle for more interesting and less predictable effects.

Beds and borders

Plants are vital for softening the edges of your harder landscaping materials and for breathing life and color into your design. Plan for them at the earliest stages by incorporating suitable beds and borders into your main scheme. Left as an afterthought, beds and borders will not work nearly as well, because like other features, their shape and size can be crucial to the overall look of the garden or patio. Sometimes you will need to make provision for growing plants in conjunction with a particular feature, such as a spot to plant the climbers that are to smother a pergola. Beds with geometric shapes, perhaps raised and edged in matching materials, are an obvious choice for patio areas and might incorporate seating areas or even a pool, but they can work equally well as part of a more formal layout. The gentle curve of a less formal border is attractive and softens the effect of any garden, but do not make it too elaborate. Mark out the shape with a length of hosepipe when experimenting with an idea on site.

Right: The regular layout of a classic vegetable plot or formal herb garden means beds are easy to maintain, while presenting a certain well-ordered charm.

Left: Disguise the boundaries of a regular plot with informal plant borders. Be sure to make them unequal in size and length to achieve a more natural effect.

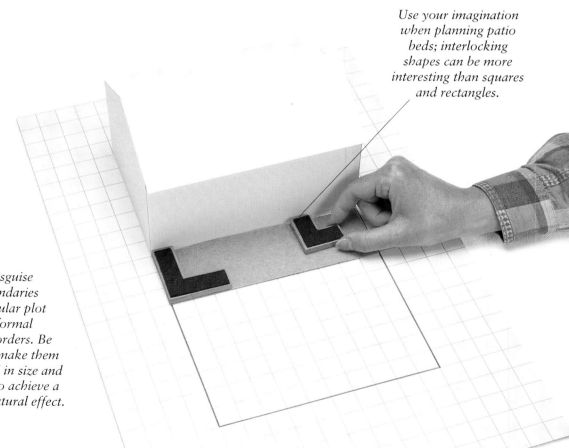

Use your imagination when planning patio beds; interlocking shapes can be more interesting than squares and rectangles.

2 Raised beds incorporated into the patio design will successfully make the link between the paved area and the rest of the garden.

1 This island bed is positioned on the diagonal to create a diamond shape. It avoids the effect of a grassy formal border that a square cut out of the lawn would have created.

Plants in borders

Consider the plants you will be incorporating into the beds, as this may influence their style and position. For example, bright annuals and scented plants are ideal for raised beds around the patio; herbs and vegetables need a good, sunny site; a pool, sculpture or seating area may require a backdrop of greenery.

A palette of annual flowers

Choosing and growing annuals is creative, it's fun and the plants are relatively short-lived and inexpensive, so you need not worry about making mistakes. You have a fabulous palette of flower types and colors at your fingertips, to be coordinated and contrasted in beds and borders, pots, tubs, baskets and troughs, and because they only last a single, if glorious, season, you can try out new combinations and effects every year. If you grow plants from seed, the choice of colors and types is even wider. You can choose exactly the shades you want and try out the latest introductions, whether that be a range of subtle pastels, double forms or interesting petal markings. Many annuals, such as petunias, antirrhinums, geraniums and impatiens, are available in a mixture of carefully selected shades, but you can also buy many single colors to mix and match your own, more subtle effects. Often a two- or three-color combination is the most effective in containers, remembering to maintain a good contrast of heights and shapes. You might go for a hot Mediterranean mix of bold primaries, a more sophisticated blend of golds and blues, oranges and creams, or simply all-white for a really special effect. Painting with plants really comes into its own if you are planning a traditional bedding scheme where the plants are arranged in geometric patterns, even letters and words, picked out in the different colors. It is vital to prepare the bed thoroughly, making sure it is free from weeds, and sketch out the design in advance, using string or a sprinkling of sand.

Carpet-forming alyssum adds lighter tones

Tiny white violas for hanging baskets and pots

Some of the larger pansies have attractive 'faces'

French marigolds - a wide range of single colors

Begonias appear in many forms and colors

Marigolds offer a range of strong colors

French marigolds - in many patterns

Brilliant orange gazanias for beds and tubs

Marigold flowers - small but plentiful

French marigolds, Tagetes, have bright green foliage and eye-catching flowers

Yellow daisylike flowers brighten up beds and borders

Impatiens - a mass of single or
double blooms
in many colors
and patterns

The color range of pansies extends
into these lovely purple shades

Densely-headed
verbena adds
strong color

Petunias are
available in
plain and
striped
colors

Alyssum is also
available in pink
and mauve color
combinations

A yellow
eye gives hot
pink begonias
striking appeal

Pansies with
strong color contrasts
add extra impact

Dahlias offer fine
petal configurations
and splendid colors

Pansies also
offer velvet textures
combined with deep colors

Above: *Unexpected contrasts of color
can be used to create a flowery focal
point, such as this splash of gold
among a sea of pinks and mauves.*

Below: *Here, the brighter colors of
mixed annuals are reserved for the
patio, while the rest of the garden is
low key with a mostly green scheme.*

Planning a pool

The light-reflecting properties of water in a pond or pool in the garden or on a patio immediately add a new dimension to your design. A pool is a natural focal point and makes a stunning, easy-care feature once installed. It also gives you the opportunity to grow a selection of exciting water plants or to install a moving water feature, such as a fountain, spout or cascade, to add sound and sparkle to the scheme. Position a pool carefully within the plot and consider the practical implications, as well as the design possibilities. Water and water plants need plenty of light and sunshine, so avoid a shady spot. Try not to position a pool too near to trees, as falling leaves can pollute the water, or too close to a boundary, where you might have construction and maintenance problems. For an informal, natural pool sketch out a rough kidney shape without too many inlets as these are difficult to construct. Alternatively, choose a more formal square, rectangle or circle, which could be raised or sunk into the ground. You might even consider two or more pools linked by a water spout or cascade to produce an interesting change of level on the patio or to link patio to garden.

Left: An informal kidney shape makes an excellent starting point for a natural pond or pool.

Left: A patio pool can be designed to fit the shape and size of an existing paved area, and raised up if excavation work is not practical.

Left: Here, a round pool takes its lead from a circular grassed area and transforms the lawn into an important focal point.

Below: *This two-level pool links the patio to the garden without looking over formal. You can enjoy the feature from many angles around the garden.*

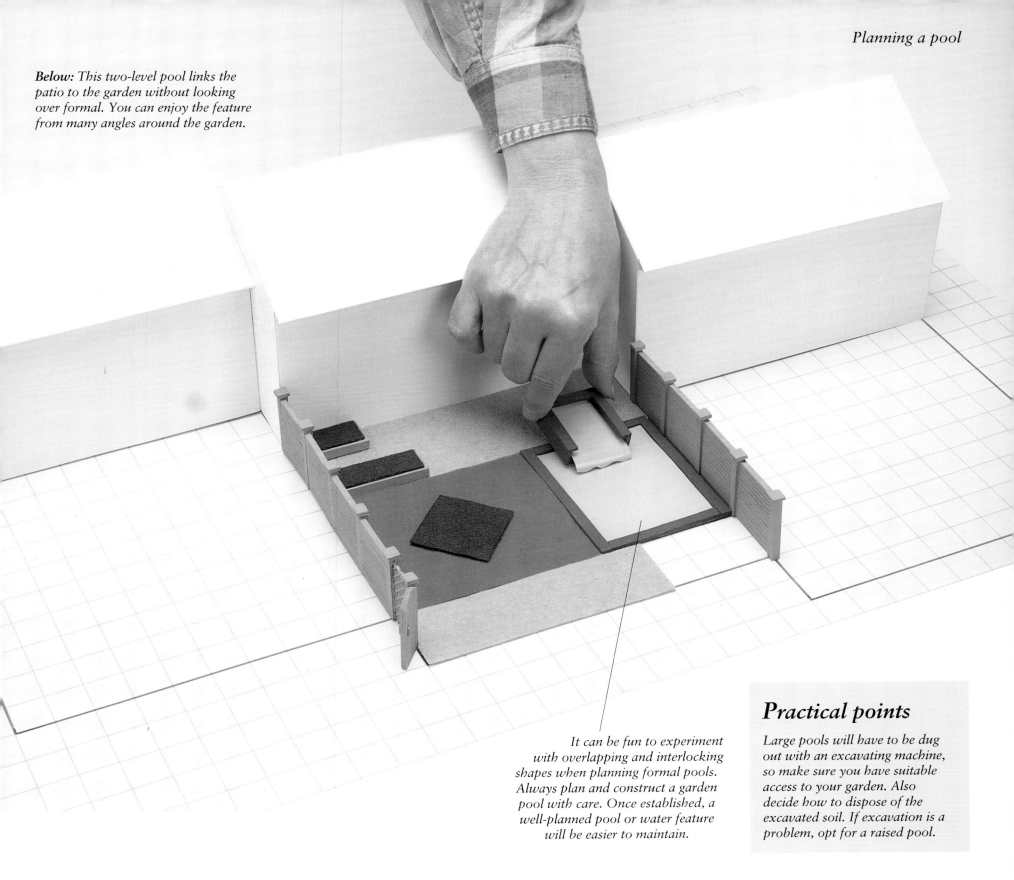

It can be fun to experiment with overlapping and interlocking shapes when planning formal pools. Always plan and construct a garden pool with care. Once established, a well-planned pool or water feature will be easier to maintain.

Practical points

Large pools will have to be dug out with an excavating machine, so make sure you have suitable access to your garden. Also decide how to dispose of the excavated soil. If excavation is a problem, opt for a raised pool.

Paths and walkways

An essential item in the garden is some form of access that remains reasonably dry and safe underfoot in all weathers and allows you to move from one feature to another. Without it, you will create unsightly tracks and the garden will become a swamp in winter. But walkways, paths and stepping stones have important design possibilities, too. They can look strictly formal, carving the plot into distinct geometric shapes, or they can meander between features creating a more relaxed feel. Because the eye naturally follows the shape and line of any pathway into the distance and beyond, the path can influence the appearance and shape of the site visually. Take it straight from A to B and the plot seems shorter, but describe a more circuitous route and the garden instantly appears bigger and more interesting, especially if you cannot see right to the end. If a solid path seems too dominant, use the broken effect of stepping stones or a staggered timber walkway. The materials you use will influence the look and feel of your garden; concrete is practical and suits the vegetable plot; stone slabs and pavers can be adapted to both formal and informal schemes. For a country cottage style, lay brick in ornamental herringbone and basketweave patterns, or for a woodland feel, lay down a path of wood chips with log slices as stepping stones.

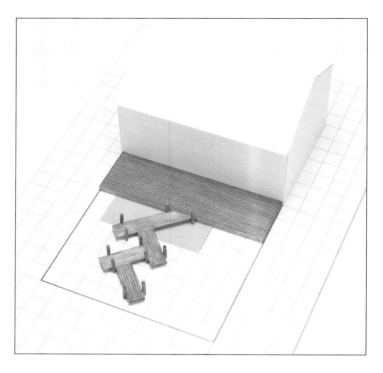

Above: A staggered timber walkway running from a patio or timber-decked area is stylish and simple to install. It is also a clever way to deal with the problem of a sloping garden.

Left: A strict framework of concrete or paving slab paths will immediately divide your garden into a formal arrangement of planting beds that may appear uncompromising but has a pleasing symmetry.

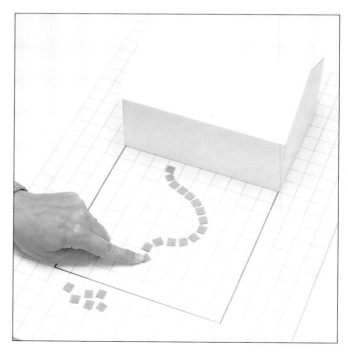

Left: A less formal route, created using stepping stones, can make the same size and shape plot look and feel completely different. This type of path cleverly distracts the eye away from the true, straight boundaries of the garden.

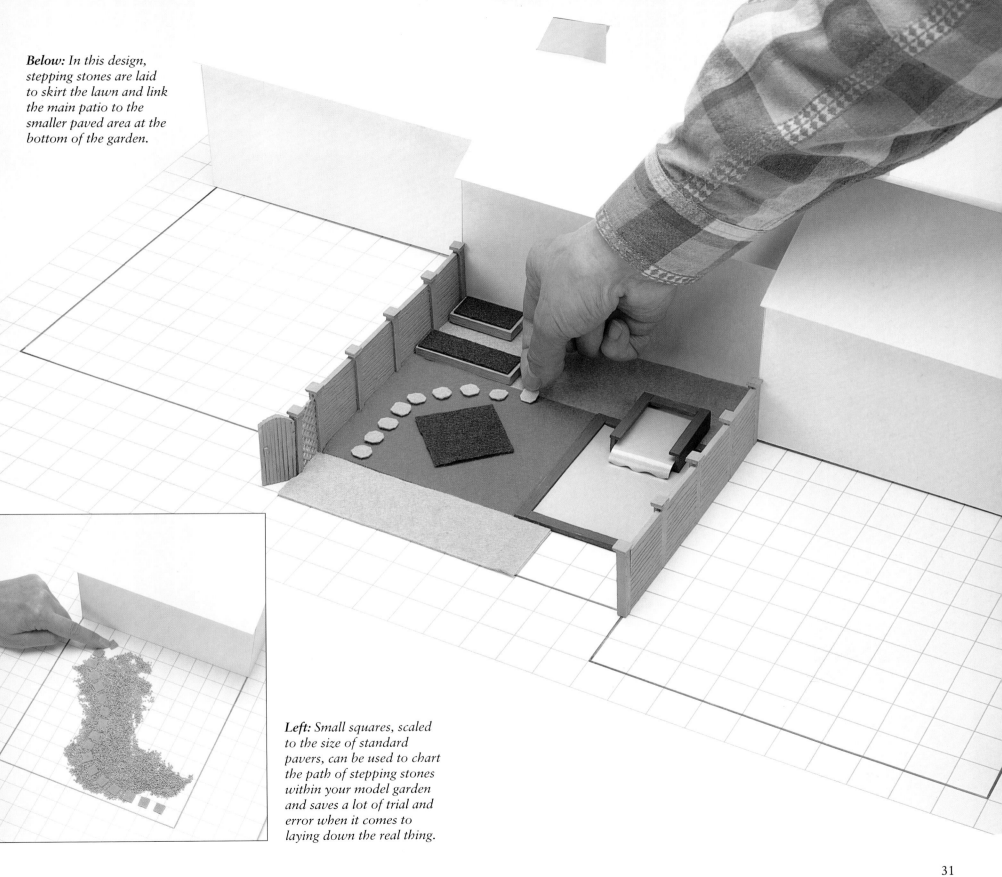

Below: In this design, stepping stones are laid to skirt the lawn and link the main patio to the smaller paved area at the bottom of the garden.

Left: Small squares, scaled to the size of standard pavers, can be used to chart the path of stepping stones within your model garden and saves a lot of trial and error when it comes to laying down the real thing.

Trellis and screening

Trellis and screens might be considered rather functional pieces of garden apparatus - they shelter, they hide, they provide support for climbing plants. But they can work magic, too: clever illusions that will transform gardens both large and small into places of interest and intrigue. Use them to disguise features you would rather not see, such as an ugly fence, the shed or utility area, or to divide the plot into more interesting, secluded areas or 'garden rooms'. These might have a special theme, such as an oriental garden, a single color scheme, a place for meditation or an area of particular seasonal interest, such as a winter garden. If you are going to smother the structure in plants, something basic, such as diamond trellis panels, should be fine, providing you select a type strong enough to take the weight of your proposed plants. Along a boundary, for weighty climbers, or where the trellis might have to withstand strong winds, go for the stronger panels, which are often the same size and strength as fence panels, and erect them in the same way as you would a fence. You can buy a wide range of ornamental styles from gothic to oriental, in different finishes, such as natural stain or colored varnishes.

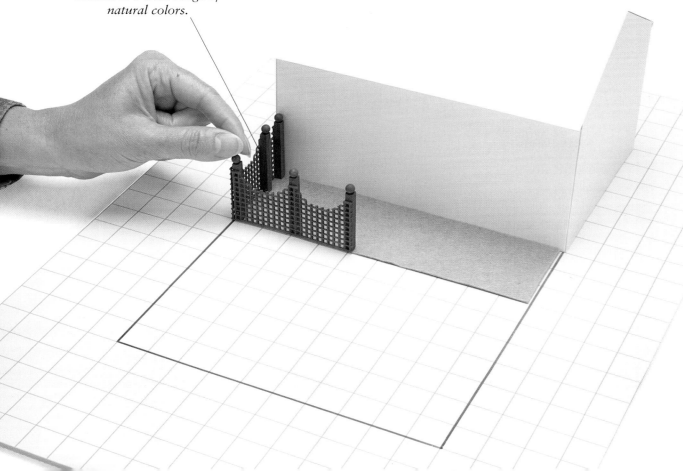

Above: Simple plant supports can be used to add height and interest anywhere in the garden. These wired posts are ideal for cordon fruit trees.

Trellis can be painted or stained in a wide range of natural colors.

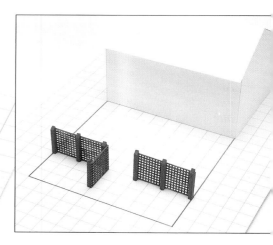

Above: Use standard sections of trellis to divide the garden into more interesting areas, each with its own theme or particular atmosphere.

Left: Sturdy or ornamental trellis might shelter a patio from unpleasant drafts or create a private area where you can relax in seclusion.

Screening the garden

Screens are less substantial or durable than trellis panels, but make excellent cover-ups that will last reasonably well for five to ten years, depending on type. Screens made from bamboo or reeds are sophisticated, if not very strong, and are perfect for creating an oriental atmosphere in the garden. Wattle hurdles conjure up a more rustic feel and make a good natural background for most plants and garden features. They can be free-standing, fixed to stable posts at regular intervals, or attached to an existing wall or fence as a cover-up.

Above: *By breaking up the plot into individual sections, you make it more interesting, limiting both what can be seen and the pace and route you must use to walk around it.*

Right: *Even a small garden might benefit from being divided into a series of garden rooms in order to add an air of secrecy and surprise to the general scheme.*

This extra panel creates a totally secluded 'room' reached by a narrow entrance.

Arches and pergolas

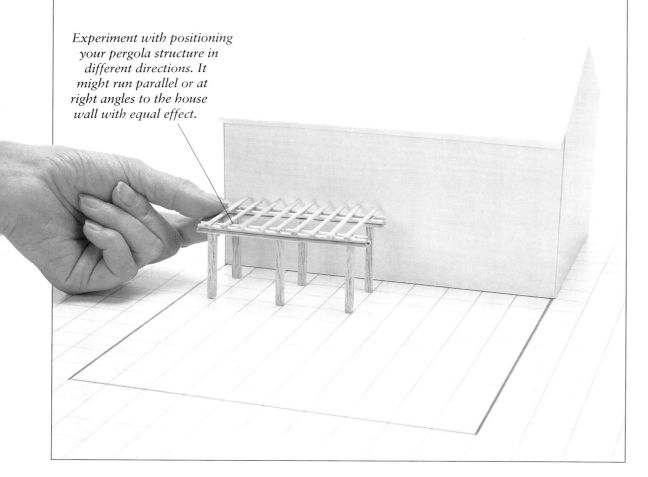

Above: *A series of arches makes a delightful feature and a wonderful flowery walk when the framework is covered in a profusion of plants.*

Experiment with positioning your pergola structure in different directions. It might run parallel or at right angles to the house wall with equal effect.

An archway or pergola not only provides a useful support for attractive climbing plants, but also adds height and a new dimension to the garden or patio by creating an ornamental entrance or walkway. This naturally encourages you to pass through it and also frames the area of garden beyond. Archways come in many guises, from rustic-style poles clothed in sweet-scented roses or honeysuckle to more formal timber shapes or ornamental, wrought metal. A series of simple metal hoops can be most effective bordering a patio or part of the garden once it is festooned with leaves and flowers. A pergola serves a dual purpose: it might be used as a walkway to lead from one part of the garden to another or to show off a particular group of climbing plants, such as a wisteria walk. It can be erected as an attractive form of shelter or shade over the patio or similar seating area, using a selection of leafy climbing plants or pull-over bamboo screens to protect you from strong sunshine and light summer showers. Again, the materials used in construction will dictate the look of the feature and affect the whole atmosphere of the patio or garden. You can use larch or chestnut poles for a rustic feel or sawn timber for a more formal scheme, maybe in conjunction with brick pillars to match nearby hard-landscaped features. If the site is a windy one, you could infill the sides with bamboo screens, lattice fencing or even vertical or diagonally arranged boarding to keep out the worst of any drafts.

Left: *A pergola might adjoin a building or be totally free-standing in order to shade a paved or patio area. Plants or screens will protect diners from strong sunshine or light showers.*

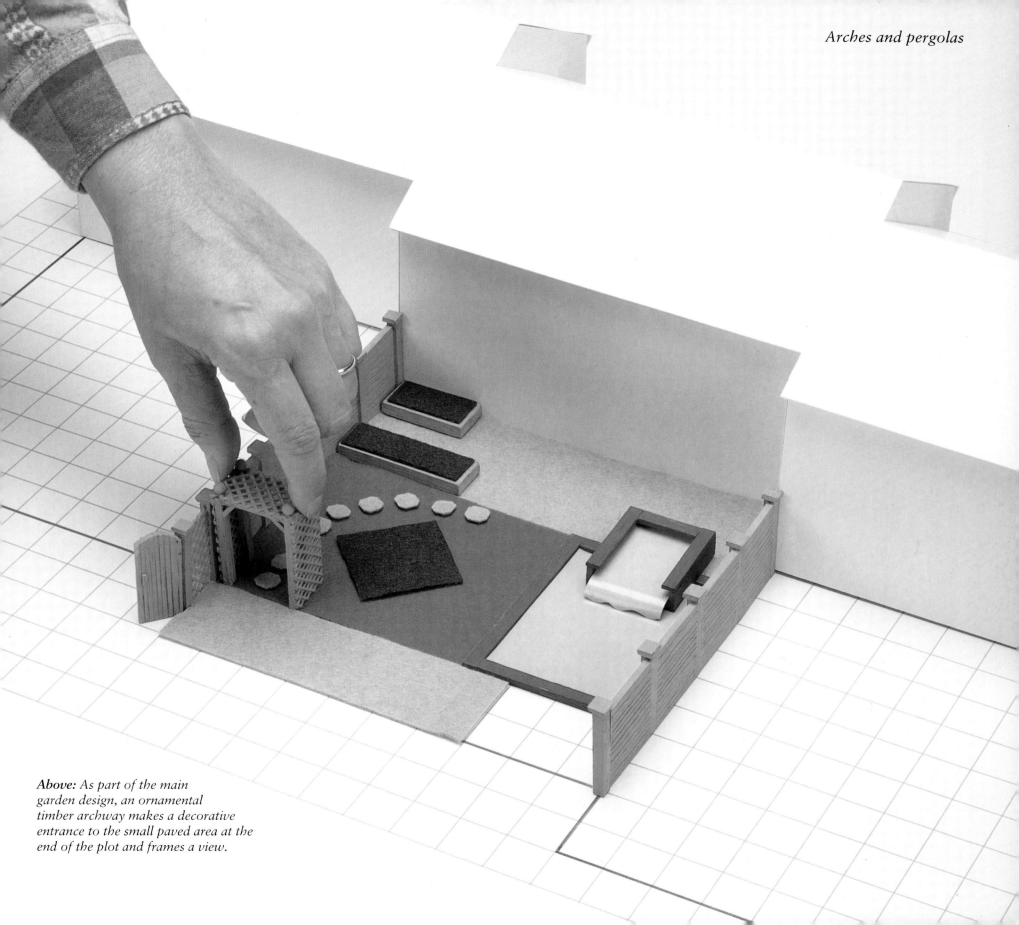

Above: As part of the main garden design, an ornamental timber archway makes a decorative entrance to the small paved area at the end of the plot and frames a view.

Positioning trees

Trees are essential to your background planting scheme, providing height and a sense of maturity even to the most modest garden. If you do not have the space or the time to wait for a proper leafy backdrop, you could always plant a small single specimen tree in a strategic position - preferably one that can offer spectacular spring blossom, fine summer foliage, glorious fall color and interesting winter fruits all in the one species. Alternatively, miniaturize the look in a formal garden with a pair of clipped evergreens in pots on either side of steps or an ornamental seat. Even dwarf conifers have their place, providing height and winter interest in containers around the patio or in the rockery. Larger gardens can enjoy larger-scale effects, such as a leafy screen or backdrop to provide total seclusion, a shady bower or an elegant avenue. When planning trees, always allow for the true spread and height of each species, so that it will neither be cramped by other features nor likely to create a nuisance or hazard to nearby buildings or a pond. A wall-trained tree should not be planted any closer to the wall than 12in(30cm) to ensure stability and soil fertility. Some areas will prove unsuitable for planting trees because of an existing drainage system or too shallow a soil with a layer of impenetrable rock below. Here, growing the trees in raised beds or containers may be the answer.

Above: Do not plant a tree any closer to a building than its ultimate spread. Cutting branches will spoil its shape and produce a lopsided effect.

Below: At the rear of the garden, trees do not interfere with anything else and make a fine view or a leafy backdrop for other garden features.

Below: Where you are planning a group of trees, odd numbers often create a better effect than even ones. Try for a range of heights and canopy shapes within the group.

Above: *Do not site trees close to a pool or pond, where shade and falling leaves can be a problem, causing green scum and pollution in the water.*

Above: *Keeping water features clear of the tree's shadow will save you time and trouble, as plants and water need light if they are to function properly.*

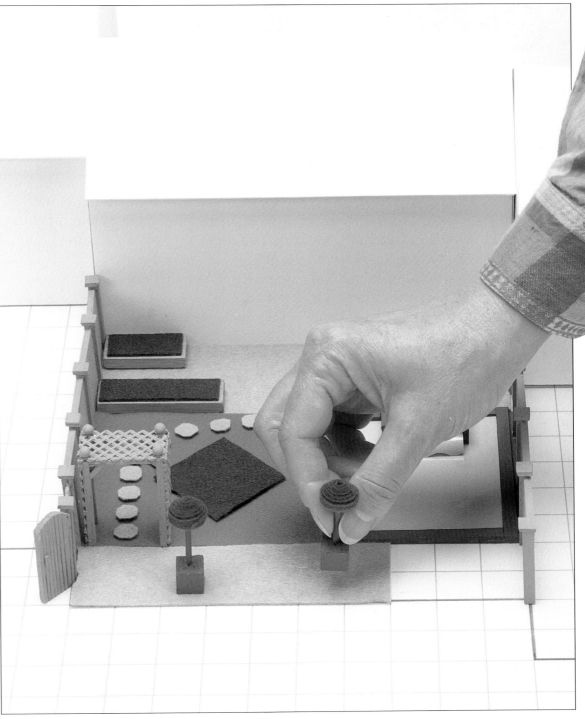

Above: *In this small, semi-formal garden, with large areas given over to water and paving for easy maintenance, the choice of trees has been restricted to a pair of clipped bay trees in decorative tubs. These add height and style to the small paved seating area at the end of the garden.*

37

Choosing designer trees

Trees need to be viewed from several different perspectives to appreciate their exciting potential within your garden design. There is the close focus on foliage shape and color, the possibility of blossom, scent, and maybe fruits or berries, too. Then there is the long view; the shape and form of the tree itself, its size and breadth, its growth habit - whether weeping, upright or spreading. Also consider what a particular species can offer your garden as the seasons change; are you looking for spring interest, summer shade or a blaze of color to lift your scheme in the fall? All these factors should influence your final decision. Initially, you will probably be most interested in the overall shape and size of your chosen trees and how they will add height and maturity to your basic framework as described on page 46. Although young trees look very much alike as saplings, each will assume a distinct shape or outline on maturity and it is important to be aware of this before you make your choice. There are tall, narrow trees, such as *Malus baccata* 'Columnaris', which are ideal where space is limited; or small dome-shaped trees to make a focal point or special feature. If you have room, round-headed forms with a spreading habit, such as the Japanese crab apple, *Malus floribunda*, can look superb and provide useful shade. If you plan a group of several trees, try to include contrasting shapes, such as columnar, pyramids or round-headed specimens.

Cytisus battandieri *is a semi-evergreen shrub grown as a small spreading tree. The summer flowers are scented.*

Crataegus laevigata 'Paul's Scarlet', *an attractive small tree with glossy dark green leaves and double red blossom in spring.*

Fagus sylvatica 'Dawyck Purple' *makes an attractive columnar tree with dark purple foliage. It reaches about 23ft(7m).*

Fagus sylvatica 'Dawyck Gold' *adds a stylish splash of gold among a backdrop of green as a special feature.*

Acer grosseri hersii, *the snake's bark maple, is a hardy tree with fine spreading branches of bright green leaves that turn red in fall. The white-striped bark is a special feature.*

Acer platanoides 'Crimson King' *makes a fine spreading tree with deep purple foliage that turns orange in the fall, thus making a fine feature for much of the year.*

Acer platanoides 'Drummondii' *adds a beautiful light effect against darker trees, with its creamy-white edged leaves.*

A tree for each season

It is a mistake to consider trees merely as a canopy or backdrop of indistinct greenery within your garden scheme, as their foliage comes in a wonderful rainbow of shades and colors. They need positioning carefully if they are to look harmonious together and with other plant material in the garden. Take seasonal changes into consideration; a blaze of hot pink spring blooms or blossom might sit awkwardly against a tree with bright yellow or golden foliage, for example. Use the more striking colors judiciously as high-lights among greener trees, but take care not to create a lop-sided effect by putting them all to one side. For an interesting backdrop, try combining different greens and creams with the occasional high-light, using trees of differing heights and shapes. Remember, too, that many deciduous trees put on a magnificent display of rich color in the fall. Choose and position such dual-purpose species with care and your garden will be alive with color and interest for most of the year.

Planted in the right position, Prunus 'Pink Shell' is only one of many beautiful flowering cherries that will put on a spectacular spring display.

Castanea sativa, the sweet chestnut, makes a beautifully spreading tree that needs plenty of space. Yellow fall color.

Sorbus aria 'Lutescens' is a good choice for smaller gardens, offering as it does spring, summer and fall interest within a single tree.

Aesculus hippocastanum, the horse chestnut, is generally chosen for its wide spreading branches, large, dark green leaves, and double flowers in spring.

Alnus glutinosa *'Imperialis' is a slow-growing variety of the common alder. It has particularly attractive, deeply cut foliage.*

Carpinus betulus *'Frans Fontaine' is a deciduous, round-headed tree with summer catkins and good fall color, followed by winged nuts.*

Betula pendula, *the silver birch, has attractive silver bark. Planting the trees in small groups emphasises the effect of the ghostly silver trunks.*

Choosing specimen trees

Some trees are so eye-catching that they make an unavoidable focal point and must be positioned carefully if you are to make the most of their visual impact. These are trees that need to stand alone, or at least among a suitable background of less dramatic companions, to show them off to best advantage. Within a larger landscape, for example, a purple beech makes a stunning highlight in a mass of greenery, where two or more trees would create a totally different, rather somber effect. For more modest gardens, there are many smaller specimen trees that can be used successfully to create an exciting focal point, say in the center of a lawn, at the end of a vista or at a particular season of the year. These trees may have attractive foliage, beautiful bark, superb spring blossom, brilliant end-of-summer color, a fine shape or an interesting habit. Some species can offer two or even several of these attributes, making them especially 'garden worthy' and ideal for smaller gardens. Many such trees have been specially developed for this purpose and although they may be expensive to buy, they will amply reward you with a suitably compact habit and special decorative qualities.

Sorbus sp. Harry Smith 12799 *is a good choice for smaller gardens looking for a tree with long season interest.*

Sorbus cashmiriana 'Pink' produces pink flowers in early summer, followed by clusters of berries.

Sorbus *x* hybrida '*Gibbsii*' *makes a fine display of cut-edged leaves in summer.*

Sorbus '*Chinese Lace*' *has particularly fine feathery foliage.*

Malus *'Butterball'* prefers a sunny position, where it makes a fine specimen tree.

Prunus subhirtella *'Flore Pleno'* makes a fine display of blossom.

Prunus subhirtella *'Autumnalis Rosea'* produces semi-double, pink-flushed flowers in mild winters.

Malus *'Director Moerland'* can offer attractive flowers, fine fruits and colorful foliage.

Laburnum *x* watereri *'Vossii'* is grown for its hanging racemes of large yellow flowers in early summer.

Fagus sylvatica *'Aspleniifolia'* is a variety of beech distinguished by its deeply cut foliage.

Some choice trees

Flowering cherries, Prunus *sp., provide a breathtaking display of blossom in spring, while Japanese maples offer wonderful foliage shape and color. Do not forget trees with interesting fruits: the mountain ash, for example, has pretty feathery foliage graced by sprays of orange or yellow berries, while the useful crab apples,* Malus *sp., have a fine compact shape, beautiful spring color and attractive, edible fruits. Other small trees that make a fine focal point include the wedding cake tree,* Cornus contraversa, *and, of course, the spectacular magnolia.*

Planning a rockery

You may have an interesting slope or hummock to plant up, or perhaps you want to introduce a little height and variety, and use up a mound of excavated soil from building a patio or pool. A rock or alpine garden is a natural and highly attractive option, but make sure that the proposed site is away from the shade and invasive roots of any nearby trees and that it is well drained, with access to plenty of light and sunshine. The ideal site should slope gently in the direction in which the sun shines at midday, with shelter from prevailing winds. In a small garden, perfection may not be possible, but do try to avoid drafty or shady areas. The feature should look in keeping with its surroundings, so do not make it too steep and view it from every angle to check that it blends in with adjoining features. A rockery always looks particularly good as the backdrop to an informal pool, especially if you incorporate a small waterfall into the feature.

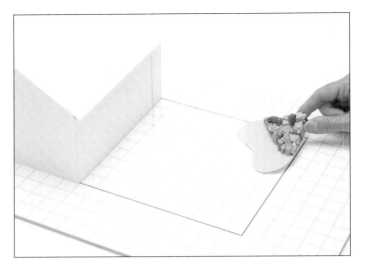

Above: A rockery, complete with a waterfall using a pump and concealed liner, makes the perfect natural backdrop behind an informal pool.

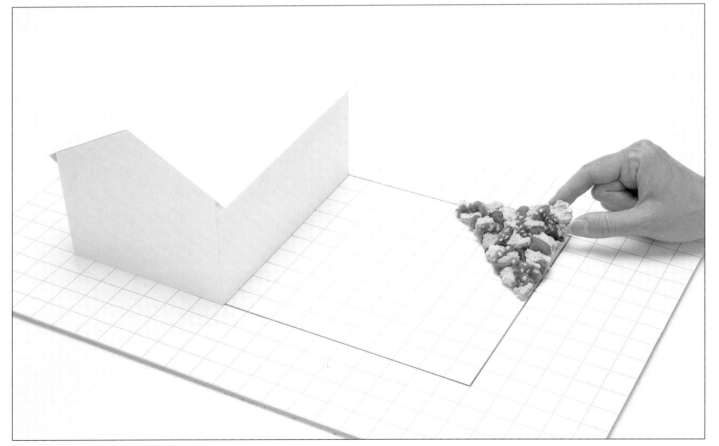

Left: A larger alpine feature can add height and an interesting change of level to an otherwise dull site, and offers the chance to display a wide selection of attractive plants.

Small rockeries

If the site just does not have the space or potential for a rockery, then create a smaller alpine feature, such as a paved or gravel scree garden, with suitable plants between the slabs or pebbles; or convert an old porcelain sink into a miniature rock garden by disguising it with hypertufa - a mixture of equal parts by volume of cement, gritty sand and peat, which sets like stone. With a good layer of rubble for drainage (about 3in/7.5cm), and a free-draining, sandy potting mix, a few boulders and gravel mulch, it will be the perfect setting for a few of your favorite alpines.

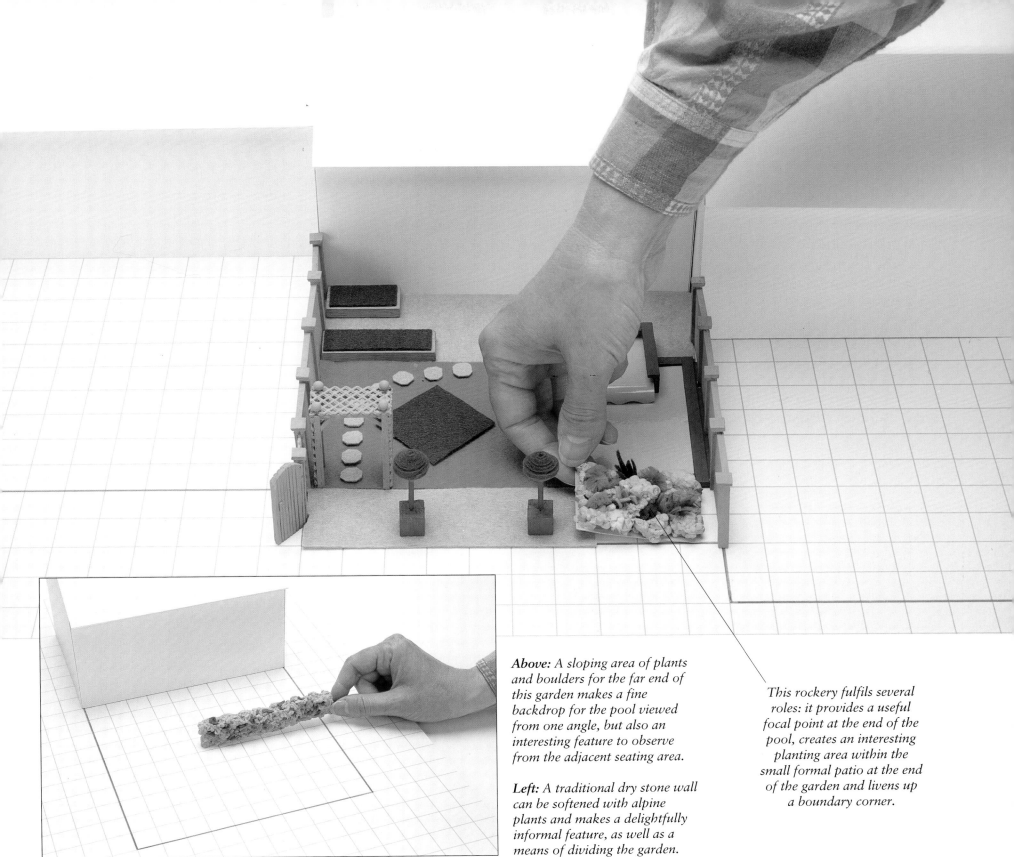

Above: *A sloping area of plants and boulders for the far end of this garden makes a fine backdrop for the pool viewed from one angle, but also an interesting feature to observe from the adjacent seating area.*

Left: *A traditional dry stone wall can be softened with alpine plants and makes a delightfully informal feature, as well as a means of dividing the garden.*

This rockery fulfils several roles: it provides a useful focal point at the end of the pool, creates an interesting planting area within the small formal patio at the end of the garden and livens up a boundary corner.

Finishing touches

With the plan finished and all the major hard landscaping features in place, you now have a good idea of how your garden is going to look and work. What comes next will be the ornaments, plants and flowers that add color, texture and interest to your scheme. You can see how the model garden has taken shape; even without plants and finishing touches, the garden has been transformed. Clever shapes and the siting of major features distract from the boundaries and create several alternative focal points around the garden: an extensive pool area, a well-equipped patio close to the house, a small lawn and a further seating area at the opposite end of the plot. Now it needs something to soften those hard edges and add some individuality and interest. Decorative pots, tubs and other ornamental containers are invaluable for positioning plants around the patio and other paved areas, and can be used to great effect to soften steps, paths or pool surrounds. A sundial, sculpture or birdbath adds interest to a dull corner or creates a focal point on the patio or in the center of the lawn.

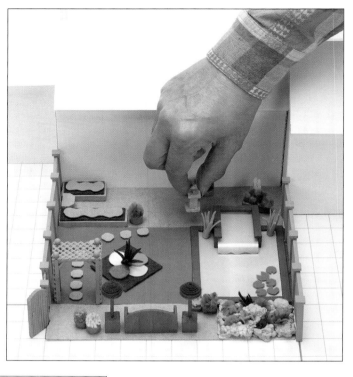

Above: Adding the finishing touches can be fun. Try to keep the style of containers, ornaments and furniture in keeping with the general theme or atmosphere you have tried to create.

Left: The finished plan can be assessed to see if the features fit together well and whether they work on a practical level. Now is the time to change any details you are not happy with before the real construction work begins.

Remember that you can buy ornaments and decorative accessories that have been specially adapted for pools and water features.

Right: The garden that started life as a dull and rather limited square plot is going to be smart and stylish, with a wide range of easy-to-maintain features in a surprisingly small area.

Coping with a narrow garden

It is a typical town or terrace garden: the long narrow strip, bordered on either side by walls or fences, often with no access other than through the house or across a neighbor's garden, which can make bringing in bulky materials and machinery difficult. The first thing to do is to break up the length of the plot in some way and get rid of that tunnel effect. You can do this by dividing the garden into new areas or outdoor 'rooms', using screens or trellis covered in climbing plants, so that part of the garden is hidden from view. This garden shows a more traditional layout, and the problem is tackled slightly differently, by providing something of special interest at the far end of the plot, which not only shortens the focal length of the overall view, but also helps to give an impression of width. The design avoids any straight lines, especially down the length of the site, which would only serve to emphasize the limited boundaries. Traditional flower borders follow a curvaceous profile and are broken on the one side by an informal pool that makes an important focal point and adds a sense of breadth in the center of the plot. Rather than a path to link the patio area, which would only introduce longitudinal straight lines, stepping stones follow a more random course. Trees are always useful for making a tall, natural screen to disguise the true length of a garden. Here, a specimen tree screens part of the end patio. The generous, gently curved patio near the house provides a convenient and stylish seating and eating area.

Below: Clever use of curves and strategically placed focal points distract attention from the length and narrowness of this typical problem site.

Terraced houses can cause garden problems. Plots tend to be narrow and access to the garden is often limited.

With neighbors on either side, boundary fences must provide privacy and security, yet make an attractive background to a long garden plot.

A major feature at the end of the garden helps to square up a narrow shape and provides a diversionary focal point.

Decorative close-boarded fence panels provide shelter and privacy around the patio. A good alternative would be stout trellis covered in evergreen creepers.

A paved area provides a clean, dry approach to the house and somewhere to sit in all seasons. Colored paving slabs, a pattern of bricks or random stone would all be appropriate here, depending on how formal you want it to look.

A pleasant grassy area winds its way down the garden following the course of informal flower borders, yet still maintains an easy-to-mow lawn with no awkward corners.

An informal kidney-shaped pond is a good opportunity to introduce an area of lush planting and exciting moisture-loving species with their dramatic variety of foliage shapes.

Informal beds planted with colorful perennials create a seasonal display to view from various angles of the garden.

Curves and undulations soften and disguise the hard lines of the plot.

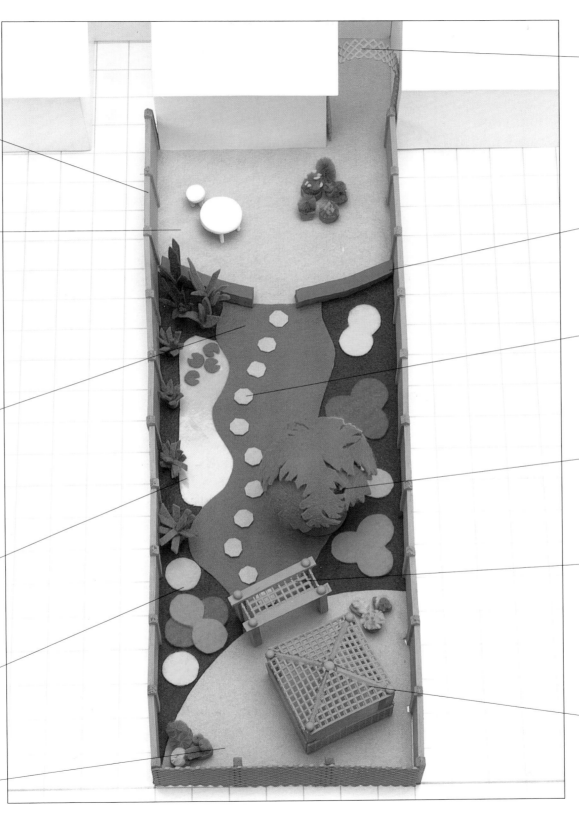

A decorative arch makes a feature out of an awkward side passage and helps to conceal the utility area.

A low wall makes a natural boundary between patio and garden without obscuring the view and adds a slightly formal touch. You could use bricks or blocks to match the paving surface.

Stepping stones have a far less formal appearance than a path. Use up any paving units left over from building the patio.

A small specimen tree creates a useful focal point as well as height and seasonal interest. A Japanese maple, a crab apple or a dogwood would all be suitable.

This pergola makes a leafy entrance to the lower patio and also links the planting areas.

An ornamental gazebo on the second patio adds height and interest in a position where most gardens have run out of inspiration. It makes an excellent focal point and a shady place to sit and view the garden from a new angle in hot weather.

Garden design on a grand scale

In many ways, a large garden is more difficult to design than a small one. There is all that space to fill without the limitations imposed by a restrictive shape and size. The way to tackle it is not to be overwhelmed by the scale of the task, but to divide the plot into new, more manageable areas and then to deal with each one in turn. If planned carefully, these areas should interconnect to form a logical whole, making an attractive and interesting environment to explore and enjoy. Here, a large water feature provides spectacular views and reflections from the house, and an extensive decked leisure area overlooks the water and includes a hot tub and comfortable seating. Hidden from the rest of the garden is a well-organized herb and vegetable plot to supply a keen cook with home-grown ingredients. A second patio beneath a large pergola offers shady seating and a separate barbecue and eating facility.

Below: This extensive site includes many exciting and practical ideas, yet it is not difficult to maintain. Distinct areas are cleverly interlocked to give the site a strong identity as a whole.

Thinking big

If you plan a pool, make it a large one, maybe on several levels and incorporating, say, a fountain, falls or water sculpture. Include islands or a boggy marsh area in a large informal pond. On an extensive patio area try changes of level, plus a range of seating and storage. A change of materials over large areas adds variety and interest.

A small specimen tree makes a fine focal point in an otherwise dull corner and provides something of seasonal interest against the boundary fence.

The pergola shades a seating and barbecue area that is paved and slightly raised to give an interesting two-deck effect.

Different fencing options provide variety and interest around a large site.

The large ornamental pool creates a stunning but easy-care feature, with year-round interest close to the house.

A group of existing trees was retained to create a mature backdrop and the opportunity to plan an interesting display of shade-loving plants.

50

Below: *The general scheme for this large country house is simple, but sophisticated - a garden designed to be enjoyed with the minimum of hard work.*

A hot tub or spa adds a new dimension to patio living and can be used all year round.

A moss and rock garden planted with lush shade-loving plants complements nearby trees and the gravel surface and livens up a shady corner.

The garden shed and a small compost heap are hidden out of sight from the rest of the garden, but are conveniently close to the kitchen door.

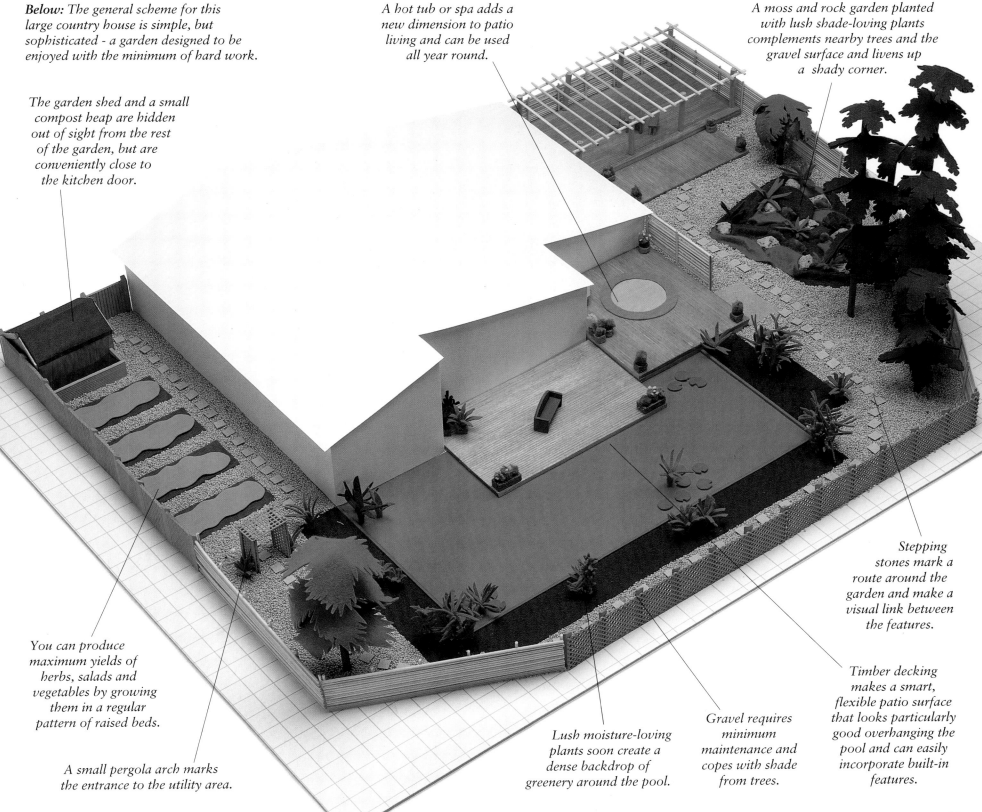

You can produce maximum yields of herbs, salads and vegetables by growing them in a regular pattern of raised beds.

A small pergola arch marks the entrance to the utility area.

Lush moisture-loving plants soon create a dense backdrop of greenery around the pool.

Gravel requires minimum maintenance and copes with shade from trees.

Stepping stones mark a route around the garden and make a visual link between the features.

Timber decking makes a smart, flexible patio surface that looks particularly good overhanging the pool and can easily incorporate built-in features.

51

Part Two
PATIO GARDENING

A patio is often described as an outdoor room, but it is actually halfway between the house and the garden, containing elements of both. From indoors, there are the furniture, floor coverings and potted plants; while from outdoors there is the weather, which means that you need to use plants, surfacing and 'hardware' durable enough to withstand the climate.

This part of the book focuses on patio gardening, with advice on which plants to use, how to plant and care for them, and how to team them together - both with each other and with 'hard' patio fittings, such as paving and walls - to create interesting planting schemes.

Patios need not always be the contemporary style suntraps we have come to expect. The basic idea can be adapted to suit houses and gardens of very different styles, simply by using appropriate combinations of paving, screening, furniture and plants. The patio does not even have to be next to the house; if the only place that gets the sun in the evening is down the garden, there is no reason why you should not have your patio there. Conversely, if you prefer to keep out of the sun, you could create a cool shady patio - perhaps using a Mediterranean-style roof of vines.

A patio provides a unique gardening environment that makes it possible to grow many kinds of slightly tender or delicate plants, usually sunlovers, that may prove difficult or unsatisfactory when grown in the open garden. There is also the opportunity to make full use of plants in containers and beds or on walls to soften the hard lines of a patio. So, whether you use plants to decorate the patio, or the patio to house your favorite plants, you will be spoilt for choice!

Left: *A relaxing place to sit and enjoy the view.*   **Right:** *An arum lily crowns a terracotta patio container.*

What makes a patio?

Patios can be made in all sorts of styles to suit their locations, but whichever you choose, the design should be inviting, easy to use and maintain, and suitable for the people who will use it. Plants on a family patio are generally easiest to manage if they are grouped together, rather than randomly dotted about, and this is also the way to make a good display from only a few plants. Most commonly, people only think of growing plants in containers or hanging baskets, but decorative though they are, there are many other options, including beds let into the paving, or made where single paving slabs have been removed. You can even grow plants in the cracks between paving slabs. Many possibilities are explored on the following pages.

Ivy is self-clinging, but will not damage a well-built wall; being evergreen, the effect remains all year - variegated kinds are colorful.

In addition to providing shelter, brickwork 'stores' heat from the sun and helps keep the patio warm in the evening. It also makes a good neutral background for colorful plants in containers.

Above: *Pots, wall planters, climbers and a patio pond with a fountain and marginal plants all add interest to a sheltered, sunny seating area that looks good, yet is quick and easy to maintain in good condition.*

Drought-tolerant alpines look good surrounded by pebbles, which act as a mulch that suppresses weeds and slows water evaporation from the soil.

Light-colored paving reflects heat and light, helping to create the 'suntrap' effect of a patio. Textured surfaces are safest in wet conditions.

Grow colorful annuals in tubs, hanging baskets and beds. When summer is over, replace them with hardy, spring-flowering plants.

Below: A patio designed for luxurious leisure time. A parasol over a table cuts down the glare if you are eating outdoors. Leave enough space around patio furniture and items such as a barbecue so that people can move around them easily and in safety.

Trellis is a useful way of enclosing a patio, providing light shade, shelter or privacy. Use it to grow climbers or hang wall planters.

Furniture is as much part of the landscape of the patio as the plants are, so choose a style that reflects that of the house and garden.

For a coordinated look keep to one style of containers and, if possible, match them to the furniture, paving or walls surrounding the patio.

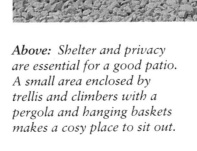

Water features on or next to a patio are very relaxing. There is always something to watch - dragonflies, fish, or perhaps a fountain. The shallow edges attract birds to drink.

Conifers and variegated evergreens planted on or near the patio provide easy-care interest throughout the year

Above: Shelter and privacy are essential for a good patio. A small area enclosed by trellis and climbers with a pergola and hanging baskets makes a cosy place to sit out.

Gravel is a good alternative to hard paving, but can be a nuisance if used close to the house, as it gets trodden indoors.

Laying slabs on sand with mortar

Preparation is the secret of sound paving - expect it to take at least as long as actually laying the slabs. Do not lay paving slabs straight onto the soil, because rain water will get under them, making the soil soft and muddy. The slabs will then sink in, wearing depressions in the soil and causing the slabs to rock. The paving soon becomes uneven and can be dangerous if the slabs tip up. To prevent this happening, prepare a proper 'base' before you lay any slabs. It need not be very deep, as a patio or path will not have to carry much weight. Start by leveling and consolidating the ground. You may need to excavate a few inches of soil for the base, leaving only the paving visible above ground. Alongside a house wall, leave a gap of 6in(15cm) between the surface of the finished paving and the dampproof course in the wall. If laying a patio, whether it be adjacent to the house or free-standing, leave the ground sloping very slightly so the water runs off it. A slope of 1in(2.5cm) in 4ft(1.2m) is all that is needed.

1 After raking the sand roughly level, smooth the surface by drawing a length of wood over it. This leaves it evenly firmed down without consolidating it too much.

A 2in(5cm) layer of rubble with 1-2in(2.5-5cm) of building sand on top makes an adequate base for a patio.

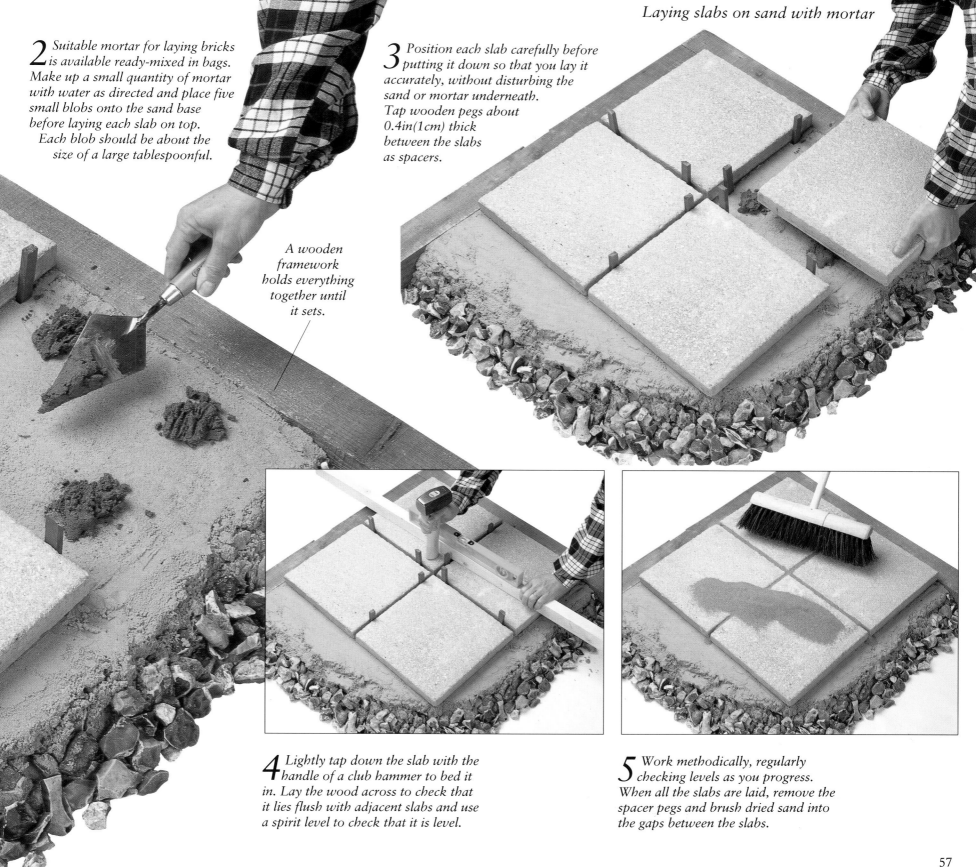

2 *Suitable mortar for laying bricks is available ready-mixed in bags. Make up a small quantity of mortar with water as directed and place five small blobs onto the sand base before laying each slab on top. Each blob should be about the size of a large tablespoonful.*

A wooden framework holds everything together until it sets.

3 *Position each slab carefully before putting it down so that you lay it accurately, without disturbing the sand or mortar underneath. Tap wooden pegs about 0.4in(1cm) thick between the slabs as spacers.*

4 *Lightly tap down the slab with the handle of a club hammer to bed it in. Lay the wood across to check that it lies flush with adjacent slabs and use a spirit level to check that it is level.*

5 *Work methodically, regularly checking levels as you progress. When all the slabs are laid, remove the spacer pegs and brush dried sand into the gaps between the slabs.*

1 *Lay the slabs a finger's width apart - you can tap in wooden pegs as temporary spacers. Brush dry mortar into the cracks.*

Make sure everything is dry at this stage so that the dry mortar runs freely into the cracks.

2 *Water briskly with a fine rose. This washes the mortar in, wets it enough so it can set, and cleans the slabs.*

Slabs on sand with dry mortar

There are some situations where fixed paving slabs are neither necessary nor desirable. If you think you may want to alter the patio layout later, perhaps taking up some slabs to make a sunken bed or pond, then it will be easier if you only have to lift the slabs. Slabs in such an area can simply rest in place while those around them are mortared down permanently. If you use very large heavy slabs, cement may not be necessary at all, especially if the patio surface will not take much weight. Even if they are not cemented down, you can still fill the cracks between the slabs with mortar to stop weeds growing. Later on you can remove the slabs with a crowbar after chipping the mortar loose; clean up the edges before reusing the slabs. Alternatively, leave the cracks between slabs open, perhaps filled with gravel, and sow rock plants between them. To prepare the site for laying slabs, proceed as described for laying paving slabs on page 56-57, using crushed rubble or ballast covered by building sand, raked firm and leveled. Leave a 6in(15cm) gap between the dampproof course in the house wall and the planned upper surface of the patio, and allow a very slight slope away from the house to deflect water during heavy rain.

3 *This method is very easy to do and leaves the slabs clean; the alternative - pushing wet mortar down between the cracks - takes ages and makes a terrible mess.*

Below: *The surface of this patio has been kept interesting by varying the pattern of the slabs and letting in the occasional block of bricks or small planting pocket, here featuring lilies and hostas. A wooden deck and steps provide a stylish change of level.*

Right: *Simple paving slabs neatly laid provide an ideal patio surface that sets off plants in beds and containers. Here, the bold, white-edged leaves of* Hosta crispula *planted in a bed alongside the patio contrast superbly with the warm tones of the slabs.*

Carefully placed containers act as focal points to break up the horizontal symmetry of a patio.

Hostas and other moisture-loving plants have their 'feet' in a damp waterside bed on the other side of the patio.

Laying bricks on sand

Laying bricks involves very much the same technique as used for slabs. Prepare the base of rubble topped with building sand in exactly the same way. The bricks can be secured in place with blobs of mortar, as shown on page 56-57 for paving slabs, except that two blobs of mortar are enough for a brick. However, since bricks are smaller and thicker and less likely to slide about or rock than slabs, they can be laid loose and directly onto the sand. This is a good idea if you think you may want to move them later - perhaps remove some to open up beds or alter the shape of the paved area. It is also rather quicker to make a hard surface in this way than when using mortar, but the result is not quite as durable. Bricks laid straight into sand are most suitable for surfacing a paved area that will not get a lot of heavy traffic over it. Since the bricks are not held in place with mortar, it is also a good idea to check them periodically and re-sit any that seem to have sunk or become uneven. This is most likely to happen in high rainfall areas or where heavy wheelbarrows, etc., are frequently pushed over the area and the weight bears unevenly over the bricks. However, used as intended, it is a perfectly good surface.

Use both hands to lift bricks straight into place. Sit them squarely onto the sand; do not drop one end or it makes a depression that will make the finish uneven.

1 Lay the base layers of 2in(5cm) of rubble and 1-2in(2.5-5cm) of building sand, as shown on pages 56-57. Rake the sand level and firm it down lightly with the back of a rake.

2 Check that the surface is level using a spirit level resting on a flat piece of wood, and smooth the surface over with this so that the sand becomes smooth and consistently firm.

3 Decide on a pattern in which to lay the bricks; these are laid in alternate pairs. Practice laying bricks on a hard surface, away from the prepared base, to gain confidence.

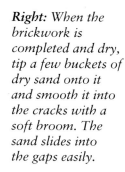

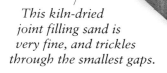

Right: *When the brickwork is completed and dry, tip a few buckets of dry sand onto it and smooth it into the cracks with a soft broom. The sand slides into the gaps easily.*

The pattern shown here is herringbone, one of the most popular and easy to lay.

4 Tap each brick lightly down at both ends with the handle of a club hammer so that it beds into the sand layer and ends up with the top completely flush with the bricks next to it.

This kiln-dried joint filling sand is very fine, and trickles through the smallest gaps.

5 As you work, check constantly with a spirit level resting on top of a length of wood to make certain that the bricks are completely level. If necessary, add or remove a little sand.

Laying bricks on mortar

A frequently used patio or path needs a hard surface that stays firm in all weathers, is non-slip when frosty or wet and will not sink or tip. It should be strong enough to withstand the weight of a loaded wheelbarrow, patio furniture, etc. - although it will not need the deep foundations required to support the weight of a car. Some of the most popular surfacing for such areas are paving slabs and bricks bedded onto mortar. Bricks create a more interesting texture than many inexpensive types of paving. You can reuse secondhand bricks from old buildings for paths and paved areas, after chipping the old mortar from them, but it is also possible to buy new bricks that resemble old ones. These are useful to create the traditional look of a cottage garden path or paving. Modern bricks are available in a variety of styles and colors to suit other schemes. Bricks can be laid in a wide range of patterns - books and magazines will give you plenty of ideas - but whichever you choose, practice first. With some patterns, even apparently simple ones, it is surprisingly tricky to place adjacent bricks right first time, especially when you are anxious to get them down before the mortar starts to set. For peace of mind, do jobs that involve concreting during spells of mild weather when it is unlikely to rain; extremes of heat or cold will affect concrete. Mortar is available in bags ready to use - just mix it with water. A slightly wet mix is easier to work with and gives you marginally longer to work before it starts to set.

3 Allow a gentle slope (1in/2.5cm in 4ft/1.2m) across the area of bricks, so that rain water runs off. If working next to a wall or the house, make sure the slope takes water away from it.

1 Surround the working area with wooden formwork nailed roughly together. Pour about 1in(2.5cm) of mortar mix over a 2in(5cm) gravel base on flattened and trampled soil.

2 Lay the first row of bricks, firm lightly down and check that the tops are level. Tap down uneven bricks with the handle of a club hammer.

Cleaning the patio

Keep the patio free of dirt and debris to deter weeds and moss colonizing it. They do not just grow in soil between slabs and bricks, but also in organic debris trapped in crevices, even over the top of cement. Clean patios with a stiff brush and warm water with a drop of mild detergent in it, or use a high-pressure hose, taking care not to blow weak mortar out from between the cracks. Do not use bleach, as it can cause discoloration. You can also use persistent path weedkillers on a clean patio in spring to prevent weed growth for the rest of the season.

4 Once all the bricks are in place, brush dry mortar mix into the gaps between the bricks. It is worth filling these hairline cracks to prevent weeds or moss invading the spaces.

5 Use a rose on the spout of a watering can to give the bricks a brief shower. This washes the mortar into the cracks and enables it to set without staining the top of the bricks.

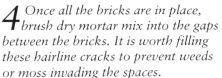

Above: Visually 'break up' a large area of paving by varying the surface pattern, texture or color. Here, a regular pattern of paving slabs has been set amongst bricks to add detail.

Left: You can create all kinds of interesting effects using bricks. Patterns such as these that echo the shape of containers or furniture on the patio can be particularly effective.

Right: Bricks, especially dark red ones, associate particularly well with plants and foliage. Where possible, use them so that plants can spill over and create pleasing contrasts.

Laying cobbles in mortar

Cobblestones make a most attractive contrast to areas of flat paving. Use them in place of an occasional slab to add a change of texture. In larger areas, they can add decorative detail or an interesting surface. Because rounded cobblestones are not very comfortable or easy to walk on, they can be used to good effect on a patio to guide people away from overhanging plants or to deter children from getting too close to a barbecue area or pond. Cobbles team specially well with stone seats and ornaments and look superb in an oriental-style area. They also make an attractive base on which to stand containers of plants, particularly shrubs - the texture of cobbles associates particularly well with subjects such as Japanese maples and conifers that have feathery foliage. When cobblestones are used as a decorative surfacing amongst plants, it is usual to bed them loosely into the soil; this allows rain water to run through, and also lets you change the design without difficulty. However, if people are to walk on the cobbles, bed them into cement or mortar to hold them firmly in place. Since they can be slippery when wet, it is also a good idea to set cobbles so that about half of each stone is above the level of the cement base, leaving plenty of drainage space for water to run away between the stones. In a large area, lay cobbles on a very slight slope, the same as for paving slabs, so that water does not lie in puddles.

Weeds and moss

Dig out weeds with a narrow-bladed knife or eradicate them using a proprietary path weedkiller. This will kill any plant it touches, so take care to keep it off plants overhanging the paving or deliberately planted in it. Remove large weeds by hand first, as woody top growth persists even after it is dead. Where there is any open soil for plants, weeds can grow, too. Do not use path weedkillers round them as they will kill the plants as well. Weedkillers will not kill moss, nor is it a good idea to use proprietary mosskillers unless they specifically state that they can be used on paving - most do not. Dig out moss with an old knife or trowel instead.

1 Make a boundary of wooden formwork around the working area and nail it together. Pour in about 2in(5cm) of rather wet mortar mix and smooth with a bricklaying trowel.

2 Choose even-sized cobbles, 2-3in (5-7.5cm) in diameter, and press them about halfway down into the mortar. Stagger the rows slightly so that adjacent cobbles fit close together.

3 Work a small area at a time. Continue adding more stones until you have filled the area completely. Try to keep the surface of the cobbles as level as possible as you work.

4 Check the level by laying a piece of wood over the top; gently tap any uneven cobbles into place with a club hammer. Do not tap the cobbles directly; they may split.

Be sure to check the level and tap down the stones before the mortar starts to set.

Left: *A decorative inset made of pebbles within a larger area of paving. Instead of being laid to give the traditional cobbled yard effect, the stones on this patio have been angled to produce a swirling pattern.*

Below: *In this oriental-style area, complete with an appropriate stone lantern, flattish stones have been laid on their sides. This creates a cobbled area that is easier to walk on than one where the stones are set on end.*

An ornamental feature in a gravel area

Gravel is the cheapest, yet one of the most attractive, paths you can have. It is also the quickest and easiest to put down or to take up and move. It is good for home security, as the crunching sound it makes underfoot gives warning of visitors. Gravel is very adaptable and looks 'at home' in a rustic cottage garden or an ultramodern 'designer' patio. But one of its best features is the way plants take to it. Seedlings quickly naturalize themselves or you can deliberately plant into it. The most suitable plants for growing in gravel are naturally drought-resistant alpines, herbs, euphorbias, and small shrubs such as cistus, helianthemum and hebe. Conifers associate marvelously with gravel, but many will go brown around the edges if subjected to drought. Junipers are the most tolerant; choose a compact variety if space is limited. Gravel can also make a stunning feature with a patio. Try leaving out a few paving slabs to create an irregular area of bed and make a planted gravel garden in the space. Team some suitable plants together, and perhaps add an ornament - it looks good, yet is virtually maintenance-free.

Laying gravel on a rubble foundation

Alternatively, gravel can be laid over a base of rubble. If you have some broken bricks or other domestic rubble, you could use this, as long as the pieces are no larger than 2x2in(5x5cm), otherwise they will 'appear' through the gravel. As some of the gravel will sink between the larger pieces of rubble, make sure that the gravel layer is at least 2in(5cm) deep so that it covers the rubble completely.

Anti-weed mulch material is a flexible plastic fabric, often sold cut to length off a roll in garden centers.

3 *To make a planting hole, sweep aside some gravel and cut a cross in the fabric, about twice the width of the rootball of the plant you are inserting.*

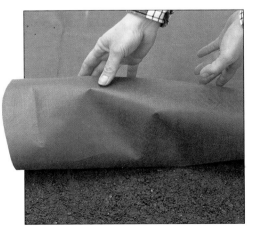

1 *After leveling and consolidating the soil, cover it with anti-weed mulch material for a maintenance-free gravel area. Simply unroll the fabric and lay it out over the ground.*

2 *When the fabric is in place, cover it with gravel to hold it down or pinion it with wire 'hairpins'. Use a rake to spread and level the gravel, making the layer 1-2in(2.5-5cm) deep.*

4 *If the soil under the gravel is good, you can plant straight into it. If it is poor, dig out a few extra trowelfuls and replace it with good-quality, soil-based potting mixture.*

5 *Make the planting hole a little larger than the plant pot. Knock the plant out and position the roots in the hole. Fill the gaps with more potting mixture and firm gently.*

7 *A small ornament completes the 'cameo'. Stone always looks well with gravel. This stone lantern has a Japanese feel about it, but a large rounded stone or a pile of smooth cobblestones would also work well.*

8 *The finished arrangement will be quite drought tolerant once the plants are established, but they will need regular watering until then.*

Juniperus x media 'Carberry Gold'

Euonymus 'Emerald 'n Gold'

Thymus 'Archer's Gold', a gold-leaved thyme.

6 *A small group of plants makes more of a feature than a single one if space permits; choose plants that complement each other and that are reasonably drought tolerant.*

1 *Arrange a group of large round stones on a base of rubble and building sand. Choose several similar stones, with one much larger and of a different color to make a contrast.*

Using stones and gravel as a decorative feature

Here, large, rounded boulders and smaller cobbles are arranged together and drought-tolerant plants added to complement them. This scheme could add interest to a large area of gravel, such as a drive, but make sure you choose a spot where it does not interfere with pedestrians or car parking. Or try it within a patio, in a square where four paving slabs have been left out. Insert the plants through the hard foundation of the surrounding area of paving or gravel. Alternatively, leave a patch of bare soil to develop as a feature when laying the patio. If you do this, cover the soil with anti-weed mulch fabric (see page 66-67), insert the plants through it and cover it with gravel. A feature like this has a definite 'front' to it and should face the direction from which it is most often seen. If it is to be seen from all round, design it so that the largest stones and tallest 'key' plants are in the middle, with smaller groups and creeping plants radiating out in a roughly circular shape around them.

2 *Lay a patch of cobbles - smaller rounded stones, all the same color - onto the sand near the main group. Try adding a plant to the group between the biggest stones.*

Junipers are the most suitable conifers to grow in gravel; this one is 'Blue Star', which grows to only about 18x18in (45x45cm).

4 *Before planting, trowel out some of the sand and rubble to reach the soil beneath. Make a hole through the sand for each plant and add potting mixture. Remove the plants from their pots and insert them in place.*

3 *Choose drought-tolerant, smaller plants to put between the smaller stones. Stand them in place in their pots while you decide on the final planting arrangement.*

68

5 Finish off by spreading a layer of fine gravel between the stones and plants. Rounded stones look best and are smoother than crushed gravel, which has sharp edges. Use just enough to cover the sand.

6 After planting, water everything well in. Although the plants used here are fairly drought-tolerant, keep them watered until they are well established and can take care of themselves.

Cotton lavender is a dwarf evergreen shrublet with feathery silver foliage. It grows to about 24x24in (60x60cm).

The gravel acts as a 'mulch', helping to retain moisture around the plant roots. It will need 'topping up' every year or two, as some sinks into the sand below.

Juniper 'Blue Star'

Lamium 'Pink Pearls'

7 When the plants have grown up a bit, they will partly obscure the stones and look as if they grew there naturally. None will need pruning, although the cotton lavender can be trimmed lightly every spring or after flowering to keep it in shape.

Viola labradorica is happy in sun or shade, and spreads slowly by seeding itself into the gravel and gaps between stones.

Santolina incana (Cotton lavender)

Acaena glauca (A low-growing New Zealand burr)

Planting in the cracks between slabs

Another way to add interest to a stretch of paving is to plant low-growing plants into the cracks. This is a good alternative to removing slabs and making beds (see pages 72-73) where space is short and you need a 'step-over' planting scheme. However, you could combine the two ideas and make a bigger and even more imaginative planting scheme. The best way to establish plants is to improve the soil and then plant or sow subjects that are suited to the conditions. If possible, improve the soil first before you lay the slabs, otherwise you will need to prise up the slabs around the cracks to work on the soil. Remove any rubble and stones and if the soil is very poor, replace some of it with good topsoil and a similar amount of well-rotted organic matter. Put any large plants in before replacing the slabs; be sure to lift the edges of the plants carefully out of the way to avoid damaging them when you replace the slabs. Alternatively, replace the slabs first and tuck smaller plants in between them. Use an old dinner fork or spoon to make planting holes in confined spaces.

Sowing seeds between slabs

Sprinkle seeds of alpine flowers, alyssum or creeping thymes thinly in the cracks between paving slabs. Do this instead of using grown plants or to fill the gaps between existing plants or for a denser planting scheme.

1 *Choose a mixture of low, mound-forming plants and compact, low, spreading plants, particularly those with aromatic foliage. Plant them in the 'crossroads' between the slabs.*

2 *Plants in small pots are easier to fit into a limited space and are also cheaper to buy. After planting, firm the soil gently around each plant.*

3 *Arrange plants of contrasting shapes next to each other. Lift out the straggling ends of trailing plants onto the slabs when you plant them.*

4 *Make each planting hole about the same size as the rootball and pop the plant into place. Planting is much easier if you leave slightly wider gaps than usual between paving slabs.*

5 *Create groups by planting several adjacent corners. In time, the plants will almost cover those slabs, so remember to leave the main walking areas reasonably clear.*

6 *Sprinkle pea-sized shingle over the cracks and tuck it under creeping and rosette plants. This provides drainage around the necks and helps to prevent plants rotting.*

Sempervivum *hybrid*

Mother of thyme (Thymus drucei minus)

Thymus 'Doone Valley'

Miniature thrift (Armeria caespitosum)

7 *Water plants and seeds in well and do not allow them to dry out during the first growing season. After that, they should be able to survive, except in unusually long, hot, dry spells.*

Planting up beds in paving

One way of livening up a large area of paving is to make sunken beds by removing occasional slabs and planting in the spaces. If you are laying a new patio, it is simple to plan for such beds in advance. Instead of laying the usual rubble and concrete base over the whole area, leave the soil clear where your bed is to go. Improve the existing garden soil (assuming it is reasonably good) with organic matter, such as well-rotted garden compost, and pave round it. If you want to take up slabs from an existing paved area, chip away the cement from between the slabs and lever them out with a crowbar. If they are completely bedded into cement, you may not be able to avoid cracking them, and you may need a power hammer to remove them, together with the foundations beneath them, until you reach bare soil. Once the slabs are out, excavate as much rubble as you can from underneath and then refill with good topsoil, enriched with some extra organic matter. You could leave the bed 'flush' with the paving, or make a low raised edge to it using bricks or rope-edged tiles.

1 Decide where you want to create a bed and stand your plants, still in pots, on the slab you have decided to remove so you can judge the effect.

2 Prise the slab out - this one is easy as it is only loose-laid over soil. Excavate the hole so there is room to put in plenty of good soil for the plants.

3 If the existing soil is reasonably good, simply add some suitable organic matter to improve the texture and help moisture retention.

5 *Planting compact rock plants in the corners 'ties in' the bed with rock plants growing in the cracks between other paving slabs nearby.*

Saxifraga 'Beechwood White'

Sedum 'Lydium'

6 *Plant all four corners for a neat, look. Choose plants that contrast in color and shape, and that will spill out over the surrounding paving.*

4 *Put the largest plant in the center of the new bed. This potentilla is compact and bushy, with a long flowering season through the summer.*

Plants for paving

Because the surrounding slabs keep roots cool and prevent evaporation, the soil dries out much more slowly than potting mixture in containers. The plants have a bigger root run, too. The following plants will flourish in paving: Acaena, Alchemilla mollis, Cistus, Dianthus, Diascia, ericas, Frankenia, Helianthemum, junipers, rosemary, sedums, Sisyrinchium, thymes & sages.

Potentilla fruticosa 'Red Robin'

Festuca glacialis

7 *Tuck some gravel around and under the plants for decoration and drainage. Use the same gravel to cover gaps in the rest of the patio.*

Ideas for plants and paving

In odd backwaters of the garden, where nobody walks about much, you can plant flowers or rock plants into the cracks between paving. Drought-tolerant plants, including some kinds of rock plants, are the most suitable for a low-maintenance scheme (see page 73). But why not try something different? Self-sown seedlings of many kinds of hardy annuals are just as drought-tolerant. If the cracks are not cemented over and there is even the poorest soil between them, these plants often just 'arrive' without ever having been sown. The best way to get self-sown seedlings going is to plant suitable plants nearby - not in the patio itself - and let them set seed. Then simply pull up any that grow where you do not want them. Even tall plants like hollyhocks can look charming growing randomly in paving next to a wall, but for a more orderly look you may prefer to plant 'tamer' species into gaps or into small beds made by removing an occasional paving slab. In this case, be sure to improve the soil under the slabs, as grown plants are less accommodating than self-sown seedlings. Creeping plants with scented foliage are particularly pleasant. They contribute their lingering aroma to the air every time they are stepped on and lightly crushed - but do not walk on them too often. Non-flowering chamomile and creeping thymes are ideal. Try growing plants that spread over the paving, such as nasturtium, but choose a situation where they will not be walked on. And as a complete change, why not plant a small area with a herbal or alpine 'lawn' made of a mixture of low creeping plants, with stepping stones to allow you to pick your way through them?

Below: You can remove the occasional paving slab in a patio and convert each area of exposed soil into a miniature bed. This is a good way of adding interest to a large expanse of paving or, as here, of fitting more plants into a 'busy' small patio.

Left: Although it is an annual, alyssum will seed itself into cracks between paving, so there is often no need to keep replanting it every year. The flowers have a light honey scent.

A mat of low-growing foliage plants makes a superb foil for taller flowering plants in this patio bed.

Left: Heat- and drought-tolerant species of alpines are a good choice for planting between cracks in a hot sunny area; use pea shingle or gravel to topdress the soil between plants.

Right: Chamomile makes a delightful scented herbal ground covering. The variety 'Treneague' is best as it does not flower and remains compact in form. Use it around paved 'stepping stones' or in cracks between paving slabs, as it is not very hard wearing.

The flowers are an attractive bonus on this variety of chamomile.

The dense leaf rosettes of houseleeks and similar plants suppress weeds between slabs.

Plants that self-seed in paving cracks

Flowering plants that develop from self-sown seedlings can create a delightfully casual, cottage garden look to any patio. The following plants will grow from seeds that germinate naturally: Alchemilla mollis, Alyssum, Antirrhinum (*Snapdragons*), Arabis, Calendula *marigolds*, Corydalis lutea *(Yellow corydalis)*, Cymbalaria muralis *(Ivy-leaved toadflax)*, Erinus alpinus, *Hollyhocks, Pansies and violas, Viola labradorica, Nasturtiums, and Wallflowers.*

Left: You can make a small bed anywhere by lifting up several paving slabs, removing the foundation underneath and replacing it with topsoil. Use these beds to blunt the sharp edges of an angular feature. Here, a pebble-strewn bed softens the outline of a circular, brick-rimmed pond.

The heather cultivars being used here need ericaceous potting mix, which the conifers will not mind.

Heathers and conifers

Nowadays, many people look for easy-care but stunning all-year-round patio displays. Evergreen plants are the basis of this type of scheme. They look good all the time, but need minimum maintenance. One of the most interesting ideas is a mixed planting scheme, which is almost a miniature garden in a tub. Some of the most suitable subjects include dwarf conifers, heathers and grassy plants. You could also add very compact evergreen shrubs, such as variegated euonymus, for variety and tuck in a few small spring bulbs or alpines for seasonal interest. One point to watch when planning this type of scheme is growth rates. A large mixed tub can soon look unbalanced if some subjects 'take over', so always check how big and how fast you can expect everything to grow. Check, too, for soil requirements. Many heathers, for example, must have a lime-free potting mix. Conifers and many evergreen shrubs will be happy in this, too, but some evergreen shrubs, such as box, prefer normal soil, so do not plant them in the same container.

1 *Select the heathers and a couple of dwarf conifers - an upright and a domed variety will look good.*

2 *Fill the tub with potting mix to within a pot's depth of the top and stand the plants in it while you arrange them. The tall upright conifer will look best towards the back of the display.*

3 *Tap the plants out of their pots and put them as close together as possible, so that the tub is well filled and looks instantly mature. Variegated evergreens add more interest.*

4 *Distribute the flowering heathers throughout the arrangement, intermingling them with the different colored foliage of the other plants.*

Notice how the contrasting shapes enhance the display.

5 *When everything has been planted, tuck a few handfuls of bark chippings in between the plants to give them a pleasing background that goes well with the wooden tub. It also acts as a moisture-retaining mulch.*

Evergreens in tubs

Variations on the evergreen theme include gold-leaved and variegated evergreen plants. Grow the larger varieties as specimens in individual tubs. In a shady garden, try evergreen ferns and variegated ivies. Box grows in shade, as long as it gets at least two hours of sun every day - a potted topiary tree would make quite a novelty.

Every two to three years, repot the whole display into new soil. Alternatively, scrape away the top 2in(5cm) of soil between the plants and replace it each spring. Deadhead occasionally, but feed and water regularly.

Erica tetralix 'Pink Star'

Acorus gramineus 'Ogon'

Juniperus communis 'Compressa'

Chamaecyparis thyoides 'Ericoides'

Erica cinerea 'Katinka'

Erica vagans 'St Keverne'

Euonymus fortunei 'Harlequin'

6 *The finished arrangement should last for several years before the plants get too big and need replacing. Clip back heathers after flowering and water in dry spells, even in winter. Evergreens can go brown if they dry out.*

77

A cottage garden feature

An old cottage - or a newer one with a cottage-style garden - would look at home with a patio paved with old stone slabs, cobbles and gravel, and mock Victorian cast aluminum or rustic hardwood furniture. Containers in a good range of sizes and made of natural-looking materiais, such as terracotta flower pots, blend in best. Small pots look good in a row along the edge of garden step or on top of a low wall - use them to grow drought-resistant sempervivums, sedums or red pelargoniums. Larger pots suit single specimen plants of fuchsia, marguerite or perennial herbs. You could also plant a mixture of colorful cottage garden annuals in big pots; these can stand alone or be grouped together with other plants. Traditional cottage garden flowers, such as spring bulbs, wild flowers (such as primroses and violets) wallflowers, pansies and stocks are good for spring color. They can be planted in spring just as they are coming into flower. A good range is available in small pots at garden centers ready for planting then.

1 *Choose plenty of different old-fashioned annual flowers and a pair of large matching clay flower pots, one larger than the other.*

Flowers for tubs

In summer, you can choose from a range of old-fashioned annuals, such as clarkia, lavatera, godetia, candytuft, calendula marigolds, larkspur, tobacco plant (nicotiana), verbena and cosmos and combine them with fuchsias, pelargoniums and penstemons to create colorful pots.
For spring color, plant polyanthus, wallflowers, bulbs, violas or primroses. Plant these in fall or in spring from pots.

2 *First plant the biggest and boldest plant towards the center back of the pot as a focal point. Use slightly shorter flowers round it.*

3 *Choose something striking and colorful as the centerpiece of the smaller pot, but allow the centerpiece of the biggest pot to dominate.*

4 *Add more flowers, working forwards from the back of the pots, with the shortest at the front. Put contrasting colors and shapes next to each other for a real cottagey look.*

5 *Finish off with a 'fringe' of low sprawling plants along the front of the arrangement - a row of this type of plant would have been used in an old cottage garden to edge the path.*

Snapdragon
(Antirrhinum
'Coronette Scarlet')

Dwarf sunflower

Mixed
snapdragons

Nicotiana 'Lime Green'

Argyranthemum
foeniculaceum

White
alyssum

Pelargonium
'Ringo
Scarlet'

6 *The displays in the two pots blend together harmoniously to become part of the same display. Keep the plants well fed and watered and deadhead regularly.*

A Mediterranean display

Patios are relatively new on the gardening scene outside the Mediterranean region, where they originated. There, long hot sunny days and low rainfall meant that instead of cultivating lawns and flowerbeds, it was more practical to have an enclosed yard with paved floor and drought-tolerant plants growing in containers made of local materials. There would also be a vine growing over pergola poles for shade. Today, anyone can create a Mediterranean-style patio at home. White walls, simple garden furniture, a vine - perhaps an ornamental one, such as the purple-leaved *Vitis vinifera* 'Purpurea' - and colorful pots of flowers are the basic ingredients. Red pelargoniums are a Mediterranean favorite, but more sophisticated flowers are just as suitable. Daisy shapes are a good choice - choose blue kingfisher daisy (*Felicia amelloides*), osteospermum or Swan River daisy (*Brachycome*). Succulent plants with thick fleshy leaves look at home here, too. Look for Livingstone daisy (*Mesembryanthemum criniflorum*), lampranthus and portulaca for flowers. Pots of ordinary cacti and succulents can stand outside for the summer for a Mediterranean look. Herbs are also traditional plants of the region. Perennial kinds, such as bay and rosemary, can be grown as specimen plants; pots of bush basil near a patio door are said to keep flies from going indoors. Larger, shrubby Mediterranean-style plants, such as bottlebrush, and potted climbers, such as bougainvillea, can also stand outside on the patio in summer, but as they are not hardy in cool temperate climates, be sure to move them to a frost-free greenhouse or sunroom for the winter. Grow annual climbers up walls and trellis - morning glory (*Ipomoea purpurea*) is very typically Mediterranean.

3 Knock each plant gently out of its pot. Carefully tease out any large roots that are coiled around the rootball, but avoid breaking up the rootball.

2 Plant into any good-quality, peat- or soil-based potting mixture. If the pot is to stand against a wall or in a corner, start with the tallest plant and put it at the back of the display.

1 Select a sufficient number of drought-resistant but non-hardy flowers and herbs to slightly overfill a terracotta pot and arrange them roughly around the container.

4 Place taller, upright plants, such as this bay tree, in the middle of the container, with lower-growing and trailing plants around the edge, so that they can spill out over the sides.

5 Distribute colorful flowers evenly. Tuck in small but dense patches of color to balance up the display's visual impact.

A Mediterranean wall basket

1 Take half a box of Livingstone daisies and plant them without breaking apart the block. Turn it so that the flowers fall over the edge of the container. Plant densely.

2 Fill any gaps around the roots with a little more of the same potting mixture. Trickle it carefully down between the sides of the container and the roots.

6 Try teaming a large planted container with a smaller one, perhaps hanging on a wall. For best results, choose pots of similar style and a complementary color scheme.

Livingstone daisy (Mesembryanthemum criniflorum)

Bay (Laurus nobilis)

Osteospermum 'Sunny Lady'

Osteospermum 'Silver Sparkler'

Osteospermum 'Pink Whirls'

Basil 'Dark Opal'

Cockscomb (Celosia cristata)

Helichrysum microphylla

A scented pot for the patio

Plant fragrances linger longest in warm, still air, so a patio is the ideal place to enjoy them. Perfumed plants fall into two groups; those with scented leaves and those with fragrant flowers. Of the two, those with scented leaves are most valuable in containers, as the effect lasts longer. Flowers tend to be over in a relatively short time. To release the scent from leaves you must bruise them very slightly, so place the container next to a door where you will brush past the plants or near a seat where you can touch the leaves. Herbs and scented-leaved pelargoniums are the best subjects, as they are reliably fragrant, yet compact enough for pots. Lemon verbena (*Lippia citriodora*), lavender, eau de cologne mint (*Mentha citrata*), pineapple sage (*Salvia rutilans*) and rose geranium (*Pelargonium graveolens*) are the best known. Scented geraniums in other 'flavors' include apple (*P. odoratissimum*), lemon (*P. citriodorum* and *P. crispum* '*Variegatum*') and orange ('Prince of Orange'). There are also various spicily scented plants. Try caraway thyme (*Thymus herba-barona*), *Salvia grahamii* (blackcurrant-scented leaves), *Rosmarinus lavandulaceus* (balsam scent), and *Nepeta citriodora* (lemon scented leaves). Pineapple mint has variegated leaves and a mild minty scent.

1 Most scented plants need freely draining conditions - clay pots and a soil-based potting mixture are ideal. Cover the drainage hole in the base of the pot with a large crock.

2 Half fill the pot with soil. Make sure there is room for the plants to stand on top of the soil leaving a 1in(2.5cm) gap between the top of the rootballs and the rim of the pot.

3 Select three scented plants that go well together, and gently tap them out of their pots. Place the first one close to the edge of the pot, turning it so that any overhanging shoots cascade over the side.

Lavender is ideal for a scented arrangement; the aromatic oils occur in the leaves, stems and flowers.

4 Place the tallest plant at the back of the container, again making sure that its rootball is pressed up against the edge of the pot so that there is room for the last plant.

A scented pot for the patio

5 Add the final plant. Choose contrasting leaf shapes, size and texture - include a variegated plant and one that has pretty flowers, as well as scented foliage.

Scented flowers for containers

Alyssum
Brompton stock
Bush sweetpea 'Snoopea'
Dianthus
Hesperis matronalis
(sweet rocket)
Hyacinth
Lavender
Some lilies, particularly
Lilium regale, auratum, 'African
Queen' and 'Mabel Violet'
Narcissus jonquilla
(jonquil)
Nicotiana 'Breakthrough'
Night-scented stock
Reseda odorata (mignonette)
Stocks
Wallflowers
Zaluzianskya capensis
(night stock)

Basil mint (An unusual member of the aromatic mint family).

Scented-leaved pelargonium 'Lady Plymouth'

Lavender 'Hidcote'

6 Put the finished display in a warm, sunny spot; in a sheltered area, such as a patio, the scent will linger longest. Avoid overwatering for maximum perfume-power, but do not let the plants wilt.

83

Planting up a patio rose

Although climbing and rambler roses can be grown on the patio, up walls and over pergola poles, they must be planted in the ground - in beds of good, deep soil. They will not do well in containers, even large ones, for very long. Only two kinds of roses are really suitable for growing in tubs, namely the patio roses and miniature roses. Patio roses are like compact versions of the larger floribundas and hybrid teas, growing to 18-24in (45-60cm) high. Miniature roses are really small, just 9-18in (23-45cm) high, according to variety, with densely clustered stems. Choose a well-shaped plant with evenly spaced branches, healthy foliage and plenty of flowerbuds. Use a large container and a good-quality, soil-based potting mixture. It is vital to keep potted roses very well fed and watered, as they are growing in a very limited volume of soil. Daily watering may be needed in summer, even if the pot is a large one. Feed every week from the time growth starts in spring until late summer, using a good liquid or soluble tomato feed - unless you can find a liquid rose feed. Prune patio roses in the same way as normal bush roses in early spring. Miniature roses do not really need any pruning apart from a light tidy-up in late spring to remove dead twigs. They are not quite as hardy as other types of rose, and are rather prone to winter damage.

3 Stand the plant in the middle of the pot, teasing out any large roots. Fill the gap around the edge of the rootball with more soil.

1 You can use either a clay or a plastic pot, but clay looks better. Cover the bottom of the pot with a good, soil-based potting mixture.

2 Tip the plant out of its pot - if it does not slide out easily, turn the pot on its side and knock the rim gently against something solid.

5 *Stand the pot on a matching saucer, which should be in proportion to the size of the pot. Choose one the same diameter as the top of the pot or very slightly larger.*

This patio rose is 'Ginger Nut', which grows to 18in(45cm).

Some roses for your patio garden

Anna Ford
Brass Ring (Peek a Boo)
Buffalo Bill/Young
Mistress (Regensberg)
Gentle Touch
Little Bo Peep
Perestroika
St. Boniface
Sweet Dream
Sweet Magic
The Queen Mother Rose

4 *Firm the soil gently down, leaving a 1in(2.5cm) gap between the top of the soil and the rim of the pot to allow for watering. Water thoroughly.*

If the potting mixture settles after watering, top it up to the correct level.

Left: *Miniature roses, such as this 'Pretty Polly', have smaller flowers but more of them, and they make more compact growth than patio roses.*

1 Give the basket a coat of yacht varnish and then line it loosely with a piece of black plastic to protect the wickerwork from the damp potting mix.

2 Half fill the container with moist potting mix or peat. 'Plunge' the exotic plants, still in their pots, into the soil.

Exotic plants in a wicker basket

Exotic plants with big bold leaves or bright colorful flowers enable you to create a striking tropical look on a patio. Take your cornflakes outdoors on a sunny morning, and it is almost as good as breakfasting in the Seychelles. Good plants to choose for exotic foliage include mimosa, albizia (the silk tree), cordyline palm (*Cordyline australis*) or chusan palm (*Trachycarpus fortunei*). For summer-long flowers, opt for abutilon, standard-trained lantana, or *Salvia grahamii*, which has blackcurrant-scented leaves and masses of floaty red flowers. You could also use exotic fruits, such as lemons, oranges and limes, and most conservatory plants. However, plants of this type are tender, and could not be left outdoors for the winter in cool temperate climates. Keep them in a slightly heated greenhouse, conservatory, sunroom or even an enclosed porch between early fall and early summer.

If you do not have suitable facilities, you can still create an exotic look using plants such as New Zealand flax (*Phormium*), hardy hibiscus (*Hibiscus syriacus*) and *Yucca filamentosa*. These are reasonably hardy when planted out in the garden, but will not be happy left outdoors in pots for the winter, as their roots are relatively exposed. Instead, either put them in an unheated greenhouse, or plunge them in soil up to the rims of their pots in a garden bed. When arranging exotics on a patio, remember that a few well-chosen large specimens will create a more jungly impression than many small ones. And make the most of ornamental pot holders for setting the scene. Rough bark or coconut fiber create the right impression. Alternatively, ordinary rough-textured log baskets or wicker baskets are the answer. Look for old cast-off ones at secondhand sales and give them a coat of yacht varnish. They will last for several years in the garden.

Cordyline australis *has dramatic foliage.*

3 Choose a mixture of large, striking plants, including both flowering and foliage kinds. Spiky foliage and large or unusually shaped flowers make a good exotic combination.

4 Put the biggest or boldest plant into the middle of the group and arrange the others around it. Tuck extra potting mix under the small pots to bring them all up to the same level, just below the rim of the container.

5 Pack as many plants as possible into the container, pressing the pots tightly together. Groups of three or five plants look better than even numbers.

6 Spread a few handfuls of bark chippings or similar mulching material around the tops of the pots. It not only looks good, but also helps to keep the plant roots cool and moist.

7 This arrangement has a maroon theme; each item has a small touch of the same color, which 'pulls together' plants that are otherwise very individualistic in appearance.

Cordyline australis

Hibiscus syriacus 'Red Heart'

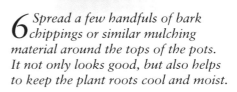

Abutilon megapotanicum 'Compactum'

These plants will thrive equally well in a peat- or soil-based mix.

1 Cover the drainage holes with a large crock, and half fill the pot with good-quality potting mixture. Knock the plants out of their pots without breaking up the rootballs.

Grasses in terracotta

Container planting schemes need not consist solely of bedding plants. One of the most unusual ideas is to use grasses and their larger relatives, such as bamboos. A large container filled with a mixture of contrasting grasses looks particularly striking in a modern setting, where the dramatic shapes really stand out well. It could also be teamed with smaller containers of evergreens, conifers and heathers to make a fuller display. They all go together very well. Ornamental grasses range in height from several inches up to several feet. The real giants, such as the tall bamboos *Arundo donax* and *Miscanthus*, are best grown in large tubs of their own once they have reached a good size. A row of these makes a good instant screen, which is portable (just) if necessary. But while they are young, they could be used for a year or two in large mixed plantings with other species. Medium-sized grasses suitable for growing on a long-term basis in containers include Bowles golden grass (*Milium effusum* 'Aureum'), *Carex comans* (an unusual bronze form of sedge which, although not a true grass, does looks like one), *Hakonechloa macra* 'Albo-aurea' (a graceful dramatically striped grass with arching gold and green leaves) and *Helichtotrichon sempervirens*, which has wide, ribbonlike, steel-blue foliage. Among the smaller grasses are many species of festuca, which have vivid blue foliage. Annual grasses - the sort grown by flower arrangers for dried seedheads - are not very suitable for containers, as they lack the impact of perennial species, unless they are grown en masse.

2 There is only just room in the pot for all three rootballs, so place each one right up against the side of the container. It is easiest to start with the largest plant.

3 Tuck the next plant in alongside the first, pushing it well up to leave room for the third. Although space is a bit tight, fill the container well for an arrangement that looks instantly mature.

4 Fit in the last plant, squeezing the rootballs slightly if necessary. Arrange any trailing leaves so that they hang over the edge of the pot and are not trapped.

5 Trowel more soil between the rootballs and firm it down slightly so that it does not sink when watered. Sprinkle a little soil over the tops of the rootballs to cover exposed roots.

Miscanthus sinensis 'Zebrinus'

6 After watering in, move the container to its final position. It will look especially good with potted specimen shrubs, particularly evergreens, or standing on gravel, perhaps in an oriental-style area of the garden.

Bowles golden grass (Milium effusum 'Aureum')

Carex comans

1 *Choose a group of three or five plants with striking yet contrasting shapes, and a set of matching oriental-style ceramic containers - you will also need some cobblestones and gravel to complete the oriental look.*

An oriental-style display

Oriental-style plant associations and containers create a patio that is quiet and restful and perfectly suited to very modern houses and enclosed courtyard gardens. It also makes a good second patio in a family garden, if you want somewhere quiet to escape. Green plants, oriental-style ceramic pots and raked gravel help to create the suggestion of a Japanese garden. Suitable plants include those with striking shapes, such as bamboo, contorted hazel and dwarf conifers. You can include flowering plants, but choose authentic ones, such as ornamental cherry. Look for a dwarf type, such as *Prunus incisa* 'Kojo no Mai' (a dwarf form of the Fuji cherry) for growing in a container. Dwarf rhododendrons, camellias, or a tree peony are also suitable. Add oriental-style ornaments for authenticity - a stone lantern, a miniature pagoda, a granite bridge over a 'stream' of gravel, or water running through a deer scarer - a bamboo pipe that 'trips' as it fills with water and taps a pot. For surfacing, try plain paving slabs or gravel raked into traditional oriental patterns, which are supposed to duplicate the patterns made in sand on a beach by the waves. Add occasional 'stepping stones' of real stone, so you can walk without spoiling the pattern with your footprints.

2 *Place curved clay crocks over the drainage holes in the bottom of each pot, then partly fill them all with a good-quality, soil-based potting mix.*

3 *Knock the plants out of their pots, teasing out some of the largest roots if necessary. Lift each plant into the center of a suitably sized pot.*

Miscanthus
sinensis
'Zebrinus'

5 Spread the gravel evenly over the area, then use the points of a hand fork to 'rake' the sort of patterns you find in an authentic Japanese garden.

6 Add a group of large knobbly pebbles or cobblestones. Press them lightly down so they stay put without looking as if they are sinking.

7 The finished display really creates an oriental look, but the plants do not require the regular trimming and wiring demanded by genuine oriental garden trees.

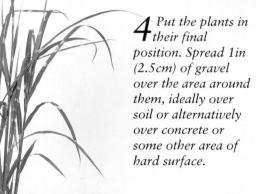

4 Put the plants in their final position. Spread 1in (2.5cm) of gravel over the area around them, ideally over soil or alternatively over concrete or some other area of hard surface.

Cryptomeria
japonica
'Spiralis'

Picea glauca
'Alberta Globe'

Part Three

WATER GARDENING

A water feature in the garden is an instant focal point; the gleam of a pond, the sparkle of a fountain or the fantastic shapes and colors of lush water plants are irresistible. Because water is so adaptable, any size, shape or style of garden can easily incorporate a stunning feature if you only have the confidence to include it in your plans, and if you take the time and trouble to plan it properly. A large plot offers the chance to enjoy a good-sized pond, complete with a wide range of plants, a bog garden, maybe a bridge or stepping stones leading to an additional platform or island area. Smaller ponds for more moderate gardens can still offer a scaled-down range of exciting plants and moving water features, such as a fountain or a waterfall. Even a tiny patio or courtyard could be transformed by a wall-mounted water spout, a small bubble fountain or a pool or bog garden in a barrel. As well as looking good, a water feature will attract a wide range of wildlife to your garden, not just frogs and toads, but also insects, such as dragonflies, different species of birds, and small mammals. A pool or coolly splashing fountain has a wonderful relaxing effect, too, converting your garden into an excellent retreat and an escape from the stress of everyday life. Best of all, once installed and providing it is correctly constructed, a water feature is one of the easiest garden features to maintain.

Left: Lilies and hostas. *Right:* Aponogeton distachyos, *the water hawthorn.*

93

Lining options

Unless you are paying a professional to design and/or excavate your pool, waterproofing it with some kind of lining material is going to be your greatest expense. There are no really cheap options: the less expensive materials will still take a fair slice of your budget, and it has to be considered that they do not perform as well as those at the top of the range. Compromising on size and style is the only way you can reasonably cut costs. Another very important point to bear in mind before you buy is that the more accurate your measurements, the less wastage there is, so do double check all your calculations. The easiest type of liners to buy are the preformed pools, which are available in a choice of sizes and shapes, including both formal and informal styles. Most incorporate a marginal shelf for plants. The cheapest of these are made of thin plastic and are fairly flimsy so do need handling and installing carefully. Their durability is fairly limited, too. Rigid pools are also available in much thicker plastic and these should last for many years. Much stronger but more expensive are the preformed GRP (glass reinforced plastic) shapes, which can be bought in an equally wide variety of styles to suit every garden.

The most popular type of liner is currently the flexible type: you buy it in a piece, or off a roll, and it stretches to fit every contour of your excavation. The inexpensive forms of PVC (polyvinyl chloride) and polyethylene (polythene) liners can be prone to fading or splitting after a few years of exposure to strong sunlight and cold winters. Several other plastic formulations are sold for pools and these are often supplied with a guarantee of up to 20 years. If you intend your feature to be permanent, you may wish to choose a butyl rubber liner, a highly durable material available in various thicknesses.

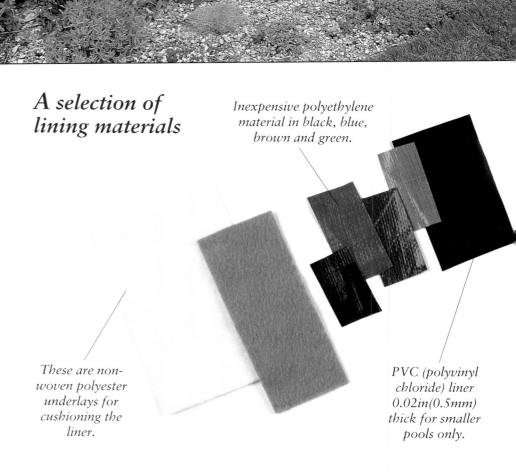

A selection of lining materials

Inexpensive polyethylene material in black, blue, brown and green.

These are non-woven polyester underlays for cushioning the liner.

PVC (polyvinyl chloride) liner 0.02in(0.5mm) thick for smaller pools only.

Left: This informal pool has been made with a rigid plastic liner. The pebble edging planted with creeping ground cover protects the pool from grass clippings.

This rigid plastic shell is typical of a wide range of preformed shapes you can buy to enable you to create an 'instant' pond in your garden.

Once installed, you can disguise the rim with an edging of your choice.

A depth of at least 24in(60cm) here will enable fish to overwinter in ice-free water.

Most rigid pool have a shelf at the right depth to support pots of marginal plants.

LDPE (low-density polyethylene) liner 0.02in(0.5mm) thick.

EPDM (ethylene propylene diene rubber membrane) 0.04in(1mm) thick. Very durable.

Butyl (isobutylene isoprene rubber) 0.03in(0.75mm) thick. Very strong and long lasting.

PVC blend with a high plasticizer content to improve flexibility and durability. Also 0.02in(0.5mm) thick.

Using concrete

Some people still favor concrete for lining a pool. It is certainly strong and can be watertight providing it is correctly mixed and applied. Concreting a pool is not a job for a novice. Even the simplest design will need to incorporate some reinforcing material. The components must be kept clean and be accurately measured, and the work carried out when there is no risk of frost or extremely dry, sunny weather.

Above A formal raised pool with a fountain makes an excellent focal point to the patio, drive or lawn.

you can edge the pool with pavers or brick to match the patio, and remember that the wide rim of coping stones makes a handy place to sit and watch the water or to stand pots of suitable plants.

Raised pools

The big advantage of a raised pool is that there is no digging and relatively little disturbance to the garden or patio. You can easily integrate a raised pool with other features, such as seating and raised beds. There may be practical reasons why a raised pool is preferable: a difficult site with bedrock just below the surface; a high water table; a sloping garden or simply a small budget. If you want to make a raised pool using a liner or a preformed unit, it is best to choose a circular or oval shape to help the pool withstand the pressure of water; without the support of soil around it, a square-edged design would be prone to splitting or breaking down at the corners. On a formal patio,

Preparing a liner pool

Mark out the shape of your proposed pool on the grass or soil using a hosepipe or pegs and string. This allows you to walk round the area and view it from every angle - even from above if you can see from a nearby window - and adjust the outline until you are satisfied it looks right. Cut turfs from the area using a sharp-edged spade, lift and roll them root side out, and keep them damp until you need them around the pool or elsewhere in the garden. Next remove the topsoil, taking care not to mix it with any subsoil or rubble, and also putting it to one side for further use. You can now begin the serious digging of the subsoil. If you have not planned to use it to contour the area around the pool or to create other raised features, arrange for the waste to be taken away. Dig out the subsoil to your required depth - a minimum of 24in(60cm) and usually no more than about 48in(120cm). Remember to incorporate a shelf for marginal plants about 10in(25cm) below the final water level. About 12in(30cm) wide should be sufficient for positioning plant baskets. Most importantly, you must make sure your excavations are completely level; if the sides vary in height, the pool will look very strange once it is filled with water. The easiest way to achieve this is to knock a 48in(120cm) post into the center of your pool area. Use this to balance one end of a straight edge extended from a series of small 12in(30cm) pegs or posts sited around the edge of the bank. Place a spirit level along the top to show you where any adjustments need to be made to ensure a level finish. When the excavations are complete and the sides are level, go over the base and sides by hand, making sure there are no major bumps or hollows, and remove any sharp stones that might damage your liner.

Above: The edge of the flexible liner is just visible at the back margin of this small informal pool. Being black helps it to blend in with the water surface.

1 *To protect the liner against damage use a custom-made pond cushioning material or use a layer of sand, old carpet, sacking or loft insulation material, as here.*

Use gloves when handling this - the fibers can irritate skin.

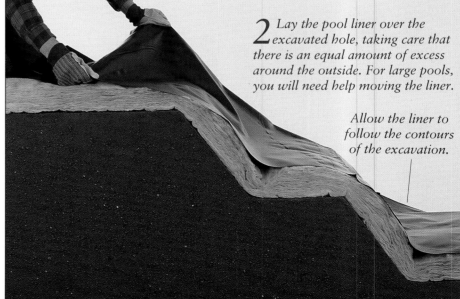

2 *Lay the pool liner over the excavated hole, taking care that there is an equal amount of excess around the outside. For large pools, you will need help moving the liner.*

Allow the liner to follow the contours of the excavation.

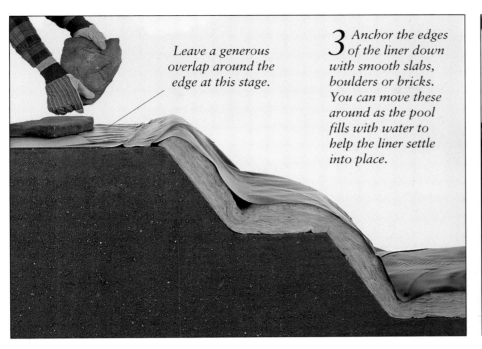

Leave a generous overlap around the edge at this stage.

3 Anchor the edges of the liner down with smooth slabs, boulders or bricks. You can move these around as the pool fills with water to help the liner settle into place.

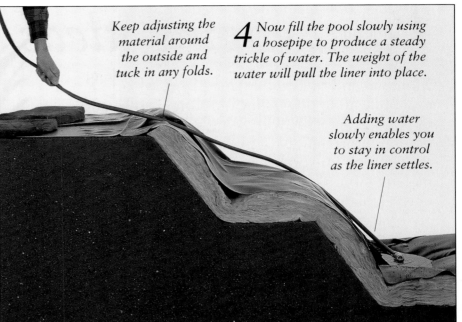

Keep adjusting the material around the outside and tuck in any folds.

4 Now fill the pool slowly using a hosepipe to produce a steady trickle of water. The weight of the water will pull the liner into place.

Adding water slowly enables you to stay in control as the liner settles.

This marginal shelf is 12in(30cm) wide with about 10in(25cm) of water above it.

5 This profile represents a small liner pool once it has been filled for the first time. This setup is used on the following pages to show edging options and how to install pumps.

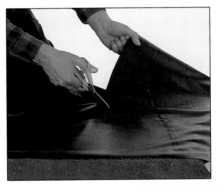

6 When the pool has filled to its level, cut away any excess, leaving about 12in(30cm) to be anchored and hidden by your choice of edging.

The maximum depth of water in the middle of the pool is 24in(60cm).

How much liner?

Add twice the maximum depth of the pool to both the overall length and width. Thus, a pool 10ft x 6ft x 2ft deep (3 x 1.8 x 0.6m) needs a liner 14 x 10ft (4.2 x 3m). Liner is flexible and stretches to fit with the weight of the water, so there is no need to allow for the gentle contouring of an informal pool or the extra few inches of a marginal shelf.

Pond edging ideas

Marginal and moisture-loving plants do an excellent job of disguising and softening the edge of ponds, especially where you want to achieve a natural informal look. But you cannot plant them all the way round; you need access to the water, maybe even a place to sit near the water's edge, where you can relax and observe plants and wildlife at close quarters. Grassy banks are perfect for informal ponds and streams being complementary to both plants and other natural materials, such as stone and timber. You could even use it in a formal way where a geometrically shaped pool is set into a lawn. The grass can be inset with other elements, such as bricks or pavers for a formal look or random stone or slabs for a more natural style. A wide flat stone close by the water's edge makes a useful seat or hard standing for a plant container, ornament or sculpture. Alternatively, add areas of other natural materials, such as a cluster of boulders interspersed with plants; well-weathered timber or railroad ties (railway sleepers) sunk into the grass; perhaps a small beach of pebbles running down into the water. If you do not have the time and patience to sow seed and wait for the grass to grow, turfs create the perfect instant effect. Ideally, you should use the turfs you have saved from your pool excavation, provided you lifted and rolled them carefully. You can also buy them commercially. Buy good-quality turfs and be sure to keep them well watered until you are ready to use them.

Above: Timber decking is an excellent and stylish companion for large pools, where it can be used to create simple platform areas, jetties, bridges and walkways. By overhanging the water, a deck not only provides the opportunity to observe fish and plants at close quarters, but also makes the pool look larger than it really is. Timber decking combines well with other materials and because it can be built to any size and shape, the design possibilities are endless.

Left: A turf edging instantly gives a completely natural look to a pool and is easy to lay. The pool liner can be tucked beneath the soil and turfs to keep it firmly anchored.

Use a wood preservative that will not harm pond life.

Left: Unless you want to create a natural sloping beach effect running into the pool, an edging of pebbles or small stones needs to be contained by wooden battens to prevent the stones spilling into the water. Use only washed stone to reduce the risk of introducing dirt or debris into the pool.

Use the larger grade of chips rather than the finer composted type.

Left: Bark chips can make an attractive edging alternative in an informal garden or woodland-type setting. Again, a wooden batten is useful to prevent the chips floating off into the water.

Use slabs that will not become too slippery if they get wet.

Left: Grass with random stone slabs is one of the most attractive options for an informal pool. The slabs can be set on sand at intervals around the edge, slightly overlapping the water to help hide and anchor the lining material.

Timber decking

Timber decking can be a quick and inexpensive alternative for pool edging. Whether raised feet or inches from the ground, it looks extremely stylish, yet is relatively easy to construct and flexible enough to create a wide range of effects. It can also be extremely useful for solving practical problems such as levelling a sloping or uneven site where building a retaining wall and backfilling would make a paved patio too expensive. Decking is also useful for linking features together, or converting a raised pool into a sunken one. The timber most commonly used for decking is a good water-repellent hardwood such as teak or oak, or one of the less expensive African hardwoods. This will require a couple of coats of preservative after installation, then an extra coat every spring or fall.

Edging with slabs and bricks

Below: *A brick border around a circular pool is quite tricky to install, but with patience the results can be stunning, as in this semi-formal pool.*

Unit paving - that is, bricks, slabs, stone setts and stones, as opposed to continuous, poured concrete - is perfect for all but the most informal pool. It provides a neat and attractive finish that remains dry and practical underfoot, and which can be satisfactorily coordinated with, or matched to, other garden features. It easily disguises the pool edges and is perfect for weighting down or hiding those liner edges. Even better, it offers an infinite variety of creative possibilities, from mixing materials to laying them in unusual patterns, or even growing creeping plants in the cracks between them. You can use just a few slabs as a pool edging or extend the plan to create a full-scale patio or seating and eating area. Bricks and pavers come in a wide variety of colors, finishes, shapes and sizes, and some are designed to interlock and create sophisticated designs. Make sure that your chosen paving is frost and rain proof. Bricks are prone to splitting or flaking, so only use good-quality paving bricks. Thorough preparation of the ground is also essential for success. The foundations must be stable - not damp and boggy - even good friable soil is too crumbly. Rocky hardcore is far better and this can be used to backfill wherever you have had to excavate unsuitable soil. Remember that the finished level is crucial, so measure the depth of layers carefully.

Cement

Sand

Hardcore

The bricks slope slightly away from the water to prevent run-off into the pool.

Left: *A brick edging needs good foundations: a 6in(15cm) layer of hardcore, 1in(2.5cm) of sand and 1in (2.5cm) of cement. By overlapping the edge of the pool slightly, the liner is completely concealed for a neat finish.*

Cement

Sand

Hardcore

Check that slabs are level at every stage using a spirit level. Make sure that the total paved area slopes slightly backwards away from the water.

Left: *Paving slabs have a larger surface area to spread the weight of the people walking on them. They need only a 3in(7.5cm) layer of hardcore to give some substance to a damp or too crumbly soil base.*

The lawn edge here echoes the informal style of the pool and provides a smooth transition to the rest of the garden.

Above: *This random arrangement of broken flagstones not only conceals the liner but also creates a delightfully informal, yet practical, hard surface around this small garden pool.*

101

Setting up a water pump

If you have sufficient depth of water, a submersible pump is a neat way to run some kind of moving water feature, such as a fountain or waterfall. The pump remains submerged below the water level, making it easier to keep both the pump and pipework concealed. Submersibles are also easier to maintain and more economical to run than surface-mounted pumps. It is very important to calculate accurately the size of pump you need or the results may be very disappointing, especially if you are hoping to run more than one feature from the same pump using a T-piece in the outlet pipe. As the head of water increases, so the output will decrease; the length of pipe, its bore and the number of bends will also affect performance. It is not a good idea to run your pump at full capacity all the time, so it is better to buy a model slightly larger than your needs. Installing the pump is simple enough, providing it is close to a convenient outdoor electrical point. This supply should only be installed by a qualified electrician.

Flow rate and head

When you start to look for a suitable water pump for your pool you will see that the specifications mention flow rate per hour and maximum head of water. Bear in mind that the widest bore tubing that you can fit to the pump will help you achieve the optimum flow rate . 'Head' also reflects the power of the pump but in terms of the height the water can be pumped to in relation to the water level in the pool. Often, the flow rate is quoted at various heads.

You can connect this foam filter directly to the pump or at the end of a plastic tube.

Geyser fountain head

Extension tube

Bell fountain head

This part of the pump casing houses a block of plastic filter foam.

These adapters allow you to connect tubing of various diameters.

This is the electric motor that drives a spinning impeller to draw in water.

Water flow control

These are two samples of clear plastic tubing that will fit this pump. Black tubing is also sold for water pumps.

Use this cap to blank off the outlet.

This T-piece allows you to divert water into two outlets.

This fountain head produces a three-tier spray of jets.

This head produces two tiers of higher jets.

Internal diameter of 25mm(1in).

Internal diameter of 19mm(0.75in).

1 An 'add-on' foam filter can improve water quality, especially where you have fish in the pool. To fit it directly to the pump take out the central pipe connecter.

The foam not only strains out particles but also harbours bacteria to break down biological wastes.

2 Push the filter firmly onto the inlet pipe of the pump. The filter is easy to take off and pull apart for regular cleaning.

You can connect the foam filter to the pump with plastic tubing if you want to position them separately.

Setting up a pump for fountain and waterfall

1 Remove the blanking cap. Push on plastic tubing to supply the waterfall. This tube has a bore of 1in(25mm).

2 Use the adjuster to control the flow of water. Fully screwed in, all the water will go to the waterfall; fully out will split the flow both ways.

Use one of the adapters to fit plastic tubing of a different diameter.

Installing a fountain

The splash and glitter of a fountain or water spout add excitement and pleasure to the smallest pool. Once you have put in the pump, installation could not be simpler; all you need is a fountain nozzle or jet, a length of plastic tubing and jubilee clips to connect them. Nozzles and jets come in a wide choice of types producing different effects, from tall plumes and multiple spray sequences, to a small bell or dome suitable for smaller pools. The mechanism might be hidden by an ornamental device, such as a human figure, a dolphin or other animal; or be skillfully incorporated into a classical or abstract sculpture. Some fountains come complete with lights and even music choreographed to the spray sequence. If you only have a tiny patio, or you have young children, you might prefer the option of a concealed reservoir where the water is recycled through a wall spout (via an old tap, a lion's head, a sculpted face or whatever you choose) into a small basin; or you could allow it to bubble over a bed of pebbles. There is something to suit everyone's taste, and style and size of garden.

Below: The fountain head with three circles of holes produces a three-tier pattern with a wide spread of water. Make sure the pool is large enough to catch the spray.

Right: Once you have fitted the T-piece into the top outlet of the pump, simply select the type of fountain head you wish to use. Most pumps are supplied with a choice of two spray patterns.

Below: This is the simplest way to provide a fountain. The submersible pump draws in water and forces it through the fountain head.

For best results, position the spray fountain head just above water level.

Control the height of the fountain by adjusting this water flow regulator.

Raise the pump on bricks to bring the fountain head to the correct level. This also helps to prevent the pump sucking in debris at the bottom of the pool.

Above: *The fountain head with two circles of holes produces a taller, two-tier pattern of water droplets.*

1 *For a geyser fountain, first fit the extension tube onto the T-piece. This will raise the head well above the water level.*

Air drawn in through these holes creates a frothy flow of water.

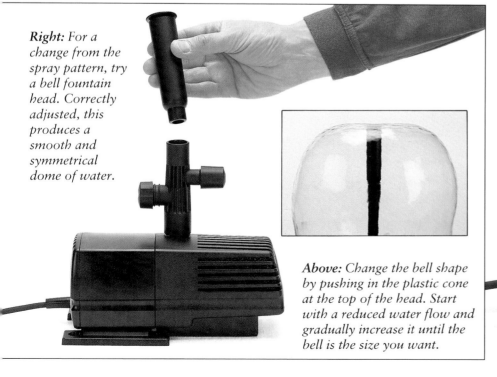

Right: *For a change from the spray pattern, try a bell fountain head. Correctly adjusted, this produces a smooth and symmetrical dome of water.*

Above: *Change the bell shape by pushing in the plastic cone at the top of the head. Start with a reduced water flow and gradually increase it until the bell is the size you want.*

2 *Push the geyser head firmly onto the extension tube. You can alter the angle of the head to create different water flow patterns.*

Above: *The geyser fountain head produces a strong jet of aerated water. To get the best effect with this head, operate the pump at its most powerful setting.*

Adding a waterfall

A waterfall or cascade is an excellent way to add movement - and, if necessary, height - to your garden scheme. It need not be large and, indeed, too tall a waterfall would require a tremendous volume of water and a very powerful pump to keep it circulating. Even a trickle from one formal patio pool into another slightly below it, makes a delightful feature. A rocky waterfall cascading over boulders into an informal pond is the perfect backdrop and a useful device to utilize waste stone and soil from your pool excavations. You will need a pump powerful enough to cope with the volume of water and the height of the falls; if you have already installed one of the larger types to run a fountain or other moving water feature, it may be possible to employ the pump to run both features by adding a T-piece to the outlet pipe. Your pump stockist should be able to advise you on the size and type of pump. If the waterfall is a big one, you may also need a top-up tank to maintain a large enough water supply. You can buy preformed fiberglass waterfalls that you can conceal behind boulders and plants to create the impression of a series of cascades.

Here the tubing has been left exposed to show where it runs. In your garden you can hide the tubing so that the water appears to spring from the stones.

The maximum size of the fountain depends on the height of the waterfall and the length of tubing involved.

Waterfall only

If you just want to run a waterfall, simply connect a suitable length of plastic tubing directly to the outlet of a submersible pump (as here) and direct the water flow as you wish.

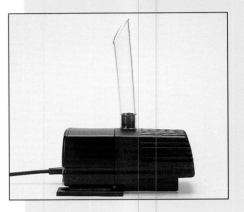

Above: *An informal style cascade built up from slabs of stone needs a liner beneath it to prevent the water soaking into the surrounding soil.*

Left: *In this setup a submersible pump supplies water to a spray fountain and a waterfall. Make sure that the pump you choose can power both outlets.*

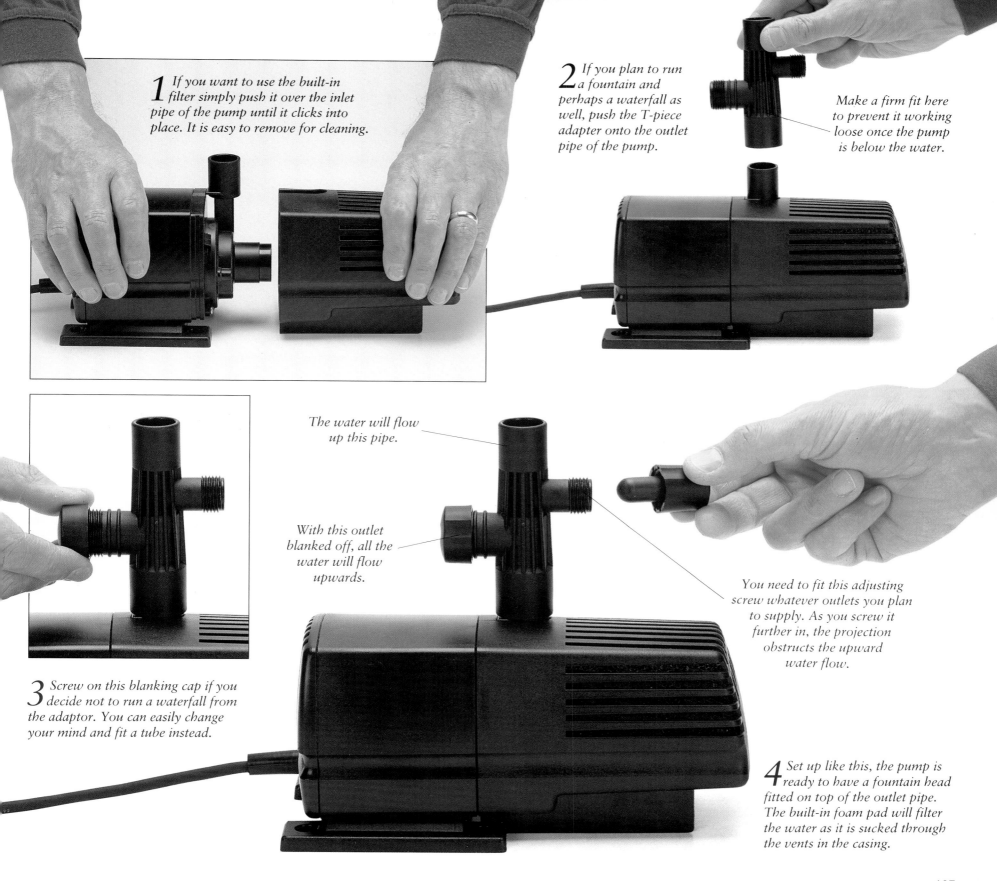

1 If you want to use the built-in filter simply push it over the inlet pipe of the pump until it clicks into place. It is easy to remove for cleaning.

2 If you plan to run a fountain and perhaps a waterfall as well, push the T-piece adapter onto the outlet pipe of the pump.

Make a firm fit here to prevent it working loose once the pump is below the water.

The water will flow up this pipe.

With this outlet blanked off, all the water will flow upwards.

You need to fit this adjusting screw whatever outlets you plan to supply. As you screw it further in, the projection obstructs the upward water flow.

3 Screw on this blanking cap if you decide not to run a waterfall from the adaptor. You can easily change your mind and fit a tube instead.

4 Set up like this, the pump is ready to have a fountain head fitted on top of the outlet pipe. The built-in foam pad will filter the water as it is sucked through the vents in the casing.

Water enters the filter here.

Water overflows through this tube if the filter floods.

Water pumped from the pool.

Water fills the bottom part of the filter and flows out here.

1 With the side cut away you can see how the pipework is arranged inside this typical biological filter suitable for small ponds up to 600 gallons (2,300 liters) in capacity.

Installing a water filter

A healthy pond relies on the correct biological balance between plants and animal life to keep unwelcome toxins and algae build-up to a minimum. In a large natural pool, nature makes its own adjustments and providing you keep rampant plants in check, you should not have any problems with green scummy water or waste materials from fish. However, in smaller pools with synthetic linings, you may need to install a water filter. This will circulate the water and keep it well-aerated and is a practical and economic consideration for small ponds. There are two main types of filter: you can recycle the water through an external system, which can be run off an existing pump, or you can install a sump at the bottom of the pool that filters the water through sand and stones or gravel via a separate pump. This usually incorporates a gauze filter pad that can be removed for cleaning. The simple filter system featured here will strain out particles of debris and suspended algae and will also reduce the levels of toxic wastes.

3 Two layers of plastic foam cover the filter medium. These strain out any debris in the water flowing from the pond.

These provide a large surface area for beneficial bacteria to colonize.

2 The bottom of the tank is filled with a biological filter medium. Here this consists of plastic corrugated pipe sections. These are inert and do not affect the water chemistry.

The top layer of foam is a coarser grade than the lower one.

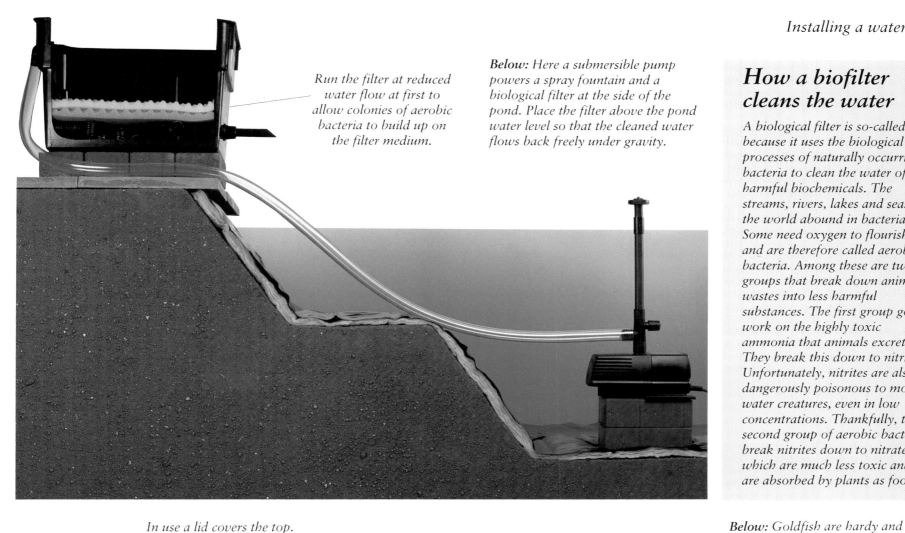

Run the filter at reduced water flow at first to allow colonies of aerobic bacteria to build up on the filter medium.

Below: Here a submersible pump powers a spray fountain and a biological filter at the side of the pond. Place the filter above the pond water level so that the cleaned water flows back freely under gravity.

How a biofilter cleans the water

A biological filter is so-called because it uses the biological processes of naturally occurring bacteria to clean the water of harmful biochemicals. The streams, rivers, lakes and seas of the world abound in bacteria. Some need oxygen to flourish and are therefore called aerobic bacteria. Among these are two groups that break down animal wastes into less harmful substances. The first group go to work on the highly toxic ammonia that animals excrete. They break this down to nitrites. Unfortunately, nitrites are also dangerously poisonous to most water creatures, even in low concentrations. Thankfully, the second group of aerobic bacteria break nitrites down to nitrates, which are much less toxic and are absorbed by plants as food.

In use a lid covers the top.

You can clean the top layer of foam without disturbing the lower one and filter medium.

Below: Goldfish are hardy and tolerant of a wide range of water conditions, but a biological filter will help to keep the pond clean and clear.

4 The filter is now ready for use. Make sure that the coarse grade of foam forms the top layer. Place the filter on a firm, level surface.

Cleaned water returns to the pond by gravity.

Aquatic baskets, liners and soil

Water plants can be planted directly into the soil or mulch at the bottom of the pool or on the marginal shelf, and with a large natural pool or lake this is often the most practical option. However, with smaller pools, using special rot-proof plastic pots and containers makes the plants - and pond - much easier to handle. A wide range of containers is available, their sides perforated to keep the soil moist and aerated. Baskets tend to have a wide base to make them stable and are usually black, which makes them virtually invisible once they are in the water. Large-weave baskets need lining with hessian or woven plastic material to prevent the soil washing away, but the containers with a close-weave pattern do not need lining. The soil you use for aquatic plants should be a rich and heavy loam to ensure that it has plenty of nutrients and remains waterlogged. A clay soil has the right consistency, but is usually not rich enough. Sandy or chalky soils are too fine and will wash out of the containers. Make sure that any soil you use is free from chemicals or herbicides.

This large plastic bowl is ideal for the more vigorous water lilies.

This type of planting basket is fine for water lilies in the early stages. Tiny perforations eliminate the need for a hessian liner.

Louvered sides prevent the loss of soil into the water.

A stout plastic bowl is ideal for small and miniature water lilies.

Most water lilies can be planted in low-sided plastic bowls such as this.

Aquatic soil

You can buy special potting mixtures recommended for water plants from garden centers and aquatic specialists. Avoid general garden potting mixtures, as these contain peat (too acidic for most aquatic plants) and soluble fertilizers. Never use fertilizers or rotted manure in the pool as they encourage the growth of algae.

The marsh marigold, Caltha palustris, a popular and dependable marginal plant.

Glyceria spectabilis 'Variegata', an attractively striped grass that grows about 24in(60cm) high.

Hydrocotyle vulgaris, a low-growing marginal.

These marginal baskets are designed to take a selection of plants and curved to fit the edge of a circular or other informal shape of pool.

Large-weave plastic container for lilies and marginals

Square fine-meshed basket for large marginals

Circular baskets with louvered sides and fine perforations are ideal for lilies and larger marginal plants. They do not need lining.

Hessian lining material

Plastic liner for large mesh containers

Water-retaining potting mixture formulated for aquatic plants.

Small stones, pebbles or gravel as a topdressing to retain soil in containers.

Mimulus luteus 'Nana', an attractive marginal plant.

A small planting pot with fine mesh panels.

111

Oxygenating plants

A selection of oxygenating plants is essential for the good health of your pool, especially if the pond is new. These are mostly submerged, or occasionally floating, species of water plants that use up waste nutrients in the water by means of their underwater foliage. This, and the fact that such plants grow prolifically, will quickly deprive bothersome algae of nutrients and minerals, and thus help to keep the water clean. Few oxygenators are as noticeably pretty as the water violet, *Hottonia palustris*, which produces a mass of pale mauve flowers above a dense underwater mat of fernlike foliage, but they generally do their job well, not only preventing green water and blanketweed, but also providing useful cover for pond insects and small fish. For the average pool, you will need about one oxygenating plant for every 2ft²(five clumps per m²) of surface area. Larger pools, over 150ft² (14m²) can reduce that requirement to nearer one plant per 3ft²(three bunches per m²). Different species flourish at different times of year, so a selection of at least two or three species is the most successful way to beat murky water.

The tiny, semi-evergreen leaves of Lagarosiphon major *(also known as* Elodea crispa*) are clustered along each stem.*

Below: Lagarosiphon major *is a perennial oxygenator that will spread into a dark green blanket of attractively curled feathery stems.*

Left: Eleocharis acicularis, *or hairgrass, is an evergreen sedge that spreads prolifically by means of rhizomes to produce a dense mat of narrow green leaf spikes.*

Oxygenators

Callitriche hermaphroditica
(C. autumnalis)
Callitriche palustris (C. verna)
Ceratophyllum demersum
Crassula recurva
Eleocharis acicularis
Fontinalis antipyretica
Hottonia palustris
Lagarosiphon major
(Elodea crispa)
Myriophyllum proserpinacoides
Myriophyllum verticillatum
Potamogeton crispus
Ranunculus aquatilis

Below: Myriophyllum verticillatum, *whorled water milfoil, is a deciduous perennial that is usually grown for its unusual and highly eye-catching mass of bright green whorled leaves.*

Hottonia palustris, *or water violet, makes a clump of feathery, light green leaves, with tall spikes of pale lilac or white flowers in summer.*

Evergreen Fontinalis antipyretica *thrives in sun or semi-shade and prefers running water, such as a stream.*

Hardy Ceratophyllum demersum, *or hornwort, grows best in cool water, where it spreads to make a submerged mat of tiny dark green leaves.*

Ranunculus aquatilis, *the water buttercup, has bright green feathery foliage that can be invasive if not kept in check.*

113

1 *One container with specially perforated sides will be sufficient for up to eight oxygenating plants, depending on the size of the pool. Use a trowel to fill it with potting mix.*

Planting oxygenators

If you have a layer of soil at the bottom of your pond then oxygenators can be simply planted by weighting the stems with a small strip of lead or some similar device such as a small stone and dropping them into the water so that they become established. However, rooted types are best planted in plastic baskets, which makes them easier to maintain. Should the plant become too rampant, you can simply lift the basket and trim back the plant as required before replacing the container in the water.

Because oxygenators grow so prolifically, especially during the warmer months, they will need keeping in check, especially at the end of the summer. As a guide, you should not allow oxygenating plants to take up more than one third of the pool's volume or they will start to become as much of a problem as the hated green strands of blanketweed. In any case, it is a good idea to thin out your plants before they start dying back for the winter. Propagating oxygenating plants is equally straightforward. If you need more young, fresh plants, simply divide the rootball into smaller pieces and pot up each plantlet.

Use the aquatic soil specially formulated for water plants.

2 *Fill the container almost to the rim. Use a dibble or your finger to make a sufficiently large planting hole for each plant.*

3 *Insert the first oxygenator into the planting hole and gently spread out the roots. Pack more potting mixture around the plant and firm it in carefully with your fingers.*

4 Continue adding the rest of the plants you have chosen, planting them in the same way and positioning them evenly around the container.

Use clean washed gravel and avoid any minerals that might affect the water chemistry.

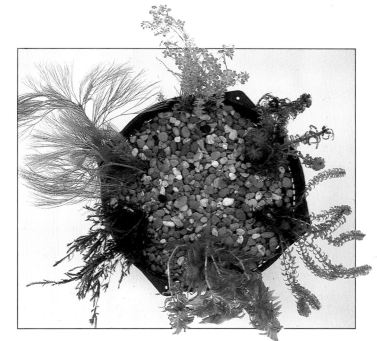

5 When all the plants are firmed in, top up the container with a layer of gravel or small stones to anchor the potting mix and to prevent fish from rooting out the plants.

Elodea crispa

Elodea canadensis

Potamogeton crispus

Callitriche hermaphroditica (C. autumnalis)

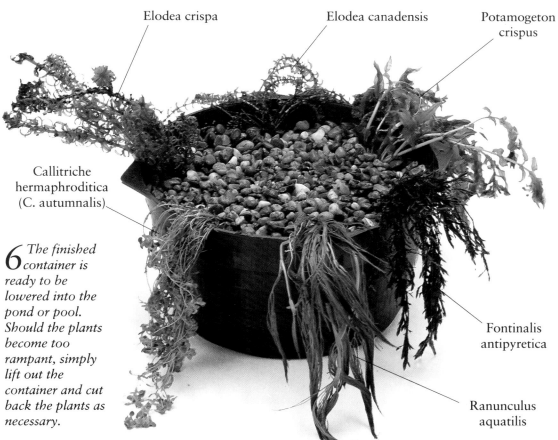

6 The finished container is ready to be lowered into the pond or pool. Should the plants become too rampant, simply lift out the container and cut back the plants as necessary.

Fontinalis antipyretica

Ranunculus aquatilis

7 Once the plants are established in the basket, they will soon start to spread out below the surface of the water in the pond.

Floating plants

Floating plants are all those that are unrooted - that is, they float on, or just below, the surface of the water. Most of them require a water depth of about 12-36in(30-90cm) and are generally very easy to install, simply by resting the plant gently on the water surface and allowing it to find its own level. Naturally, this group includes a large number of oxygenators and, like oxygenators (see pages 112-113), floating plants will grow quickly within a single season. Consequently, you may need to take them out of the water to cut them back before they become too rampant.

Floating plants, such as the sturdy and beautiful water hyacinth *(Eichhornia crassipes)* or the tiny-leaved frogbit *(Hydrocharis morsus-ranae)* not only look good but also, unlike water lilies, grow quickly and establish useful cover within months of being put into the water. For this reason, it is not generally recommended that you put prolific floating plants into very large ponds. Unless you can devise some means of removing them, such plants could quickly become a pest and dominate the entire feature.

Above: *Once it is established, perennial water hyacinth,* Eichhornia crassipes, *produces beautiful lilac flower spikes each summer.*

A selection of floating plants

Azolla filiculoides
(Fairy moss)
Eichhornia crassipes
(Water hyacinth)
Hydrocharis morsus-ranae
(Frogbit)
Lemna trisulca
(Ivy-leaved duckweed)
Pistia stratiotes
(Water lettuce)
Riccia fluitans
(Crystalwort)
Stratiotes aloides
(Water soldier)
Trapa natans
(Water chestnut)
Utricularia vulgaris
(Bladderwort)

The water hyacinth, Eichhornia crassipes, *is a glossy evergreen or semi-evergreen water plant with attractive round-edged leaves.*

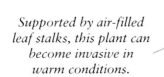

Supported by air-filled leaf stalks, this plant can become invasive in warm conditions.

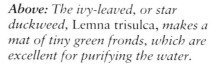

The floating annual, Trapa natans, *or water chestnut, is grown for its attractive triangular leaves, white summer flowers and edible nuts.*

Above: *The ivy-leaved, or star duckweed,* Lemna trisulca, *makes a mat of tiny green fronds, which are excellent for purifying the water.*

Above: Azolla filiculoides *comes from a family of floating water ferns that help to control pond algae. Reduce it using a net if it spreads too much.*

Below: *Planting a water soldier is simply a matter of placing it in the water. It remains mostly submerged but rises to the surface in summer.*

Above: *The hardy water soldier* Stratiotes aloides, *likes limestone waters and plenty of sun. In these conditions, it produces tiny white flowers in summer.*

Right: *Provide tropical or subtropical conditions for the shortlived, tender perennial water lettuce,* Pistia stratiotes. *Fresh green leaves grow from the center.*

Marginal plants

Varieties of Iris laevigata *include* 'Regale', *which has red blooms, and* 'Snowdrift', *which is white.* 'Atropurpurea' *has purple flowers.*

The plants that grow naturally along the banks and shallows of ponds and streams are among the most dramatic and beautiful species you could wish to feature in your garden. As a group, they include a wonderful variety of size, shape and color within the range of their foliage alone, while some have spectacular flowers, too, at certain times of the year. Even if your water feature is small, you will surely have space for one or two of these eye-catching plants, if only to feature as a focal point within your garden scheme. These plants are usually positioned on the marginal shelf, specially built just below the surface of the water, so that these mud-loving plants can keep their roots waterlogged. You can plant them directly onto the shelf in soil enriched with humus or pot them up into specially perforated plastic baskets for easy maintenance.

Marginals

Acorus calamus, Colocasia esculenta, Cyperus longus Eriophorum angustifolium Eupatorium cannabinum Geum rivale, Houttuynia cordata Juncus effusus, J.e. spiralis Ligularia dentata, Lysichiton americanus, Lysimachia nummularia, Mentha aquatica Mimulus guttatus, Myosotis scorpioides, Orontium aquaticum Peltandra virginica, Preslia cervina, Rumex sanguineus Sagittaria sagittifolia Saururus cernuus Typha latifolia Veronica beccabunga

Right: Iris laevigata *will flourish in the shallows or in the moist soil of a bog garden or pool edge. The blooms appear above the spreading clump of smooth, green, spearlike leaves in early to midsummer.*

Iris pseudacorus 'Variegata' The golden-yellow flowers appear from early to midsummer.

Iris ensata (I. kaempferi) 'Variegata'

Scirpus albescens

Above: Pontederia cordata, *or pickerel weed, is popular as a marginal plant both for its pretty blue-mauve flower spikes and its lush, glossy green leaves.*

Ranunculus flammula

Cotula coronopifolia 'Brass Buttons'

Myriophyllum proserpinacoides *(Also featured as an oxygenator)*

Planting a marginal

Marginal plants will thrive with their roots submerged in water but their foliage must be free of the water surface. It is important to plant them quickly, so that their roots and stems are exposed for as short a time as possible, and you must plant them at exactly the same level as they were in the pot or nursery bed. Remove the plants carefully from their container, but not until you have everything ready to plant, otherwise the roots may suffer. If you are planting in a bog or marsh area (you can use many marginals as bog plants), all you do is simply dig a hole about four times the size of the rootball, water the plant well and lower it gently into the hole, making sure it is at the right level. Replace the soil (enriched with organic matter if necessary) and firm in the plant. If you have a 'natural' pond with soil submerged around the edges, you can plant directly on the marginal shelf by backfilling with a suitably rich, water-retaining soil. Hold the plants in place with large rocks or boulders. For pools with 'clean' marginal shelves you can use special containers that you can lower onto the shelf and lift out for easy maintenance. These containers are available in various sizes suited to single specimens or several plants together. Curved baskets are ideal for the marginal shelf around a circular pool.

1 *Once you have assembled all the materials and plants you need, begin filling the marginal basket with moist aquatic potting soil.*

2 *Remove the marginal plant gently from its pot, taking care to support the stem loosely between your fingers.*

Keep the plants moist and in their original pots until you use them.

Make sure that the topdressing of gravel is clean and washed.

3 *Position the plants carefully in the container. Two or three plants of the same species will make a good display. Backfill and firm in.*

4 *Finish filling the container with aquatic soil and level the surface. Add a layer of gravel so that the potting mix does not float away.*

5 *The finished container is ready to be lowered onto the marginal shelf of the pond. When filled with soil, plants and gravel, it is quite heavy.*

6 *Holding the container firmly by the handles on both sides, lower it gently onto the marginal shelf without disturbing the water too much.*

7 *The marginal basket is in position on the shelf with the plants visible from the pool edge. It is easy to lift the container out for maintenance.*

121

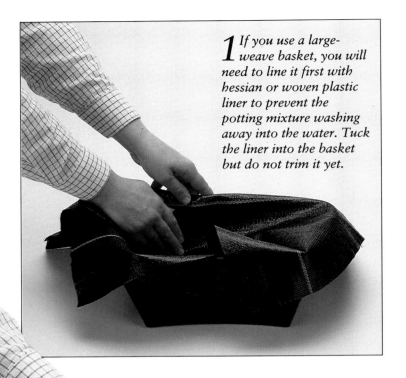

1 *If you use a large-weave basket, you will need to line it first with hessian or woven plastic liner to prevent the potting mixture washing away into the water. Tuck the liner into the basket but do not trim it yet.*

Planting a contour basket using a liner

Special planting baskets for use in pools come in a wide range of sizes and shapes to take one or several marginal or aquatic plants. Since you do not want to be fishing them in and out of the water too frequently, it makes sense to take the time and trouble to plant them up correctly in the first place. Baskets should only need lifting when plants have become too rampant and require thinning or replacing. When you have selected the correct sized basket, it may need lining to prevent the soil washing out through the perforations into the water. This also makes it easier to remove the plants should it be necessary at a later date. When it is finished, the container, complete with damp soil, plants and pebbles, will be heavy, so lower it with care; never drop it even a short distance or you will disturb the water and possibly damage your liner. Get into the water if necessary if you cannot reach comfortably by leaning over. It is important that baskets are positioned at the correct level for the plants' usual depth requirements. In deep water they may need propping up on bricks or blocks.

2 *Press the liner material lightly and evenly into the container. Now you can start filling the basket with a suitable aquatic potting mixture.*

This plastic lining material will allow water into the basket but will not rot away when immersed.

3 *Remove the plants from their pots and position them in the basket, making sure that they are at the correct planting depth and are standing upright. These are marginal plants.*

4 Carefully backfill and top up the basket with potting mixture, firming in the plants as you go.

5 Add a layer of small stones or gravel to keep the potting mixture in place once the container is submerged.

6 When the container is planted, trim away any excess liner using a pair of sharp scissors.

7 This is the finished container, lined and planted and ready to be lowered onto the marginal shelf.

Iris laevigata 'Variegata'

Zantedeschia aethiopica

Planting a water lily

Water lilies are greedy feeders, especially the more vigorous types, so they appreciate the largest container you have room for and a soil depth of at least 6in(15cm). Containers come in various types and sizes, including the familiar perforated baskets specially designed for aquatic plants, but also as wide, solid-sided bowls. Spring is the best time to transplant lilies, as they will have just started their growing season and this gives the plants plenty of time to establish themselves before becoming dormant. A reasonably mature specimen could be expected to flower in its first season, although the first blooms may be smaller and paler than expected. It is important not to cover the growing point of the lily tuber or rhizome. The crown should stand proud of the soil or gravel. Lower the heavy baskets carefully to the correct level, using bricks, blocks or upturned baskets as supports. Start young plants near the water surface - allow, say, 6-10in(15-25cm) over the crown and lower them gradually as sufficient leaves develop. As a guide, you should not be able to see open leaves below the water. It may be several years before you can fully lower deep water lilies to 3ft(90cm) or more.

1 The latest lily baskets have louvered sides with special perforations that do not require lining. Start to fill the container with a suitable aquatic potting mixture.

2 Carefully lay the lily onto the potting mixture and begin to top up the basket with more mixture, firming in the plant as you proceed.

3 When the basket is full, cover the surface of the potting mixture with gravel or small stones to keep the soil in place once the basket is lowered into the water.

The layer of small stones will also help to prevent fish from disturbing the plant.

4 *The finished container is ready to be lowered into the pool. Return the plant to water as soon as possible after planting to ensure its survival.*

Make sure that the crown of the plant is above the level of soil in the basket.

5 *Place sufficient bricks in the pool to bring the basket to the required level below the surface of the water. See plant label for planting depth.*

6 *Lower the container carefully into the water so that it rests securely on the bricks. Do not drop it in; you may damage the plant and pond liner.*

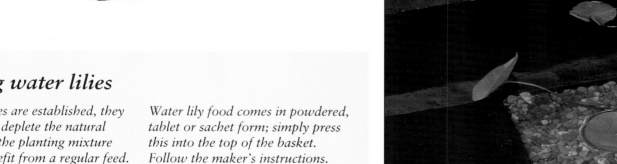

Feeding water lilies

Once the lilies are established, they will begin to deplete the natural resources in the planting mixture and will benefit from a regular feed.

Water lily food comes in powdered, tablet or sachet form; simply press this into the top of the basket. Follow the maker's instructions.

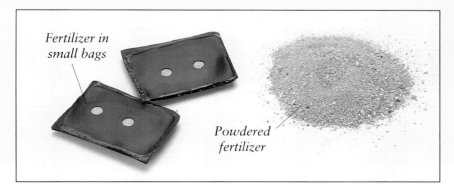

Fertilizer in small bags

Powdered fertilizer

7 *If it has been correctly planted, the lily leaves will eventually float up to rest on the water surface. Place young plants in shallow water at first.*

Moisture-loving plants

There are many interesting plants that flourish in moist but well-drained soil and they look perfect when planted to create a lush profusion of flowers and foliage near, or leading away from, the pond edge. Some are marginal plants that will tolerate damp but not totally waterlogged conditions and these can be used in either position. Many are simply hardy garden perennials that you may already be familiar with from your herbaceous borders, and that prefer a moist, rich location. Others look the part but will actually tolerate drier conditions - at least on a temporary basis. This gives you plenty of scope to devise a suitable background planting plan for your particular pond or water feature, one that will blend readily into the rest of the garden or patio design.

Below: Day lilies, Hemerocallis, bear beautiful but brief-lived lilylike flowers among deep green straplike foliage. This one is 'Pink Damask'.

Left: *Perennial* Anemone rivularis *is a good ground cover plant in damp areas. Its deeply divided green leaves are studded with white flowers with yellow centers in late spring and early summer. This plant will flourish in an area with damp soil and grow to a height of about 24in(60cm).*

Iris sibirica
'Sparkling Rose'

Primula x 'Geisha Girl'

Cowslip
(Primula veris)

Day lily
(Hemerocallis)

Primrose
(Primula vulgaris)

127

Creating a bog garden or marsh area

To create a bog garden or marsh area you need to excavate the desired area to a depth of about 14in(35cm), cover it with a large sheet of punctured butyl or other pond lining material and fill it with water-soaked soil. Ideally, there should be water standing about 2in(5cm) on the top. It is important to keep the area poorly drained and to make allowances for fluctuations in the water level according to the differing levels of rainfall throughout the year. In a naturally boggy site this is not a problem, but where you have created the environment artificially, you will need some kind of overflow facilities. This is easily installed where the bog garden adjoins a pool area by providing a few holes (about 0.5in/1.25cm in diameter) in the dividing wall. For this two-way top-up drainage system to work, the bog area should represent no more than about ten to fifteen percent of the total surface area of the pond. If there is no pond next to the bog garden, then you can install overflow facilities into a nearby ditch. The easiest way to top up the moisture levels in a dry spell is to insert a length of punctured plastic pipe at the construction stage. If you conceal the exposed end of the pipe among the plants in the bog garden you can easily trickle in more water as and when required.

Right: A bog or marsh area offers the chance to grow a selection of exciting marginal plants, such as hostas, iris, typha, mimulus, phalaris and violas.

1 *If there is not already a natural depression in the ground, begin by excavating the area to a depth of about 14in(35cm).*

2 *Roughly level the base of the hole and make sure there are no large stones or other sharp objects in the soil that might puncture the liner.*

3 *Spread the area with a large sheet of pond lining material. You can use butyl rubber or a less expensive PVC-based type of liner.*

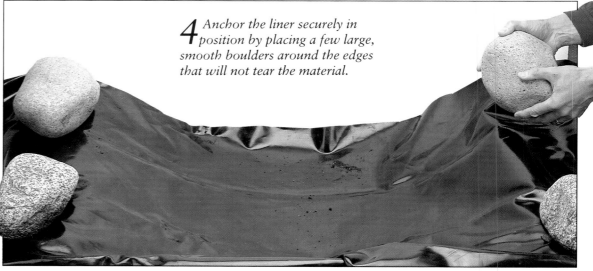

4 *Anchor the liner securely in position by placing a few large, smooth boulders around the edges that will not tear the material.*

5 Puncture the bottom of the liner a couple of times with a garden fork, so that some of the water can escape later on.

6 Spread a layer of washed gravel over the lining at the bottom of the bog area. This will help the soil to retain moisture once it is established.

7 Lay a section of perforated pipe on the gravel in the bottom of the excavation. Allow the end of the pipe to extend beyond the bog garden area and conceal it in the undergrowth.

Make irrigation holes in the pipe 12in(30cm) apart.

8 With the irrigation pipe in place, fill the area to the original ground level with a rich, moisture-retaining aquatic planting mixture.

9 Soak the ground thoroughly, so that about 3in(7.5cm) of water remains standing on the top of the soil before you start putting in any plants.

Planting up the bog garden

1 *When the soil is saturated with water, you can start to add a selection of suitable bog garden plants. There is plenty of choice.*

2 *Position the plants in the ground so that they are at the same depth as they were in their pots or nursery bed. Firm them in well.*

Here we show how to plant up the bog garden created on pages 128-129. The beauty of creating a bog or marsh area in the garden is that it offers you the chance to grow a wider range of exciting marginal plants. Or you may welcome the chance to establish a rewarding water feature without the need for expensive excavation work. Ideally, the site should be sheltered from prevailing winds with a little, but not too much, shade. The most natural position is adjoining the banks of an informal pond or pool, but if you are planning an individual bog garden, then any slight depression or poorly drained area will make an ideal site. You should try to avoid positioning your bog garden too near any tree roots as they tend to drain moisture from the soil. If your garden is small or unsuitable, you can still enjoy a miniature bog garden created in an old stone sink or barrel, providing there are three or four drainage holes and a good layer of crocks in the bottom. You can grow one or two moisture-loving plants in each container as long as you keep the soil saturated; mulching with pebbles helps to reduce moisture loss. The containers can stand on the patio or in the garden; a series of tubs containing different plants and sunk to their rims in a bed of gravel looks particularly effective. Or arrange several old sinks on the patio at various levels.

3 *Do not hesitate to arrange clumps of a single species, here Primula veris, to create an impact with more delicate-looking bog plants.*

4 *Some marginals, such as this hosta, offer wonderful shape and color possibilities simply in their foliage. Remember to protect these plants against the attentions of slugs and snails.*

5 Fill in any spaces between the new plants with washed pebbles to reduce moisture loss and create an attractive background.

6 In extremely dry conditions, you can easily top up the water level using the piece of pipe you inserted at the construction stage.

7 Aim for a variety of shape, size and color in your plants to produce an eye-catching display throughout the growing season.

Lysimachia thyrsiflora

Astilbe

Lobelia cardinalis

Primula veris

Pipe left accessible for watering

Mimulus

Mimulus

Hosta

Creating a water feature in a barrel

If you would really like a pond feature, but have no room in the garden or on the patio, or if excavations and major building work are impractical, you can always set up a miniature pool in a pot, tub or other suitable container. Providing they are scaled down, you can have all the features you set your heart on; water lilies, marginal plants, fish and even a tiny, sparkling fountain. The finished tub can be a real focal point and provide hours of pleasure for very little outlay in terms of time and money, as well as space. Any waterproof container is suitable, from a large cut-down barrel to a small terracotta or plastic patio pot. The only real proviso is that the chosen container has not been treated with any poisonous or fungicidal chemicals that might damage plants and fish. Some garden centers sell tub kits that come complete with everything you need, even a selection of plants, to be assembled at home. Alternatively, buy a ready-made bubble fountain in a stone or terracotta container, with plants and pebbles installed for an instant moving water feature.

2 Since the wooden barrel is not waterproof, the first task is to line it. Use a large piece of proper pond liner and push it firmly down inside.

3 Trim off some of the excess at this stage, but leave plenty around the edges to allow for it to settle down further as you add water and bricks.

1 These are the ingredients to make a stunning water feature in a tub. It is a good idea to set out what you plan to include in the final display before you start work. This also gives you the chance to see whether the elements will look good together.

Make sure this tube is firmly pushed into the pump.

4 Put the pump in now. This is a small, mains-powered model ideally suited to the size of the display. Place it on a brick for stability and to bring it up to the correct height.

5 Place a layer of bricks around the inside of the barrel. These will provide platforms to support the plant pots and stones. Use hard bricks sold for paving; they are more durable in water.

6 Add some cobbles to fill in the spaces between the bricks. These will help to stabilize the piles of bricks and will also stop the pump moving around once the feature is operating.

7 Add a top layer of paving bricks. These will support the large stones and plant pots of the final display. Build the bricks up in stable patterns to avoid problems later on.

8 Now add the large stones that will form the visible part of the feature. Rounded boulders such as these not only look attractive but will also stand continuous immersion in water.

9 Add water until it reaches the base of the boulders. This will leave enough expansion room to add the plants and final stones.

133

Planting up the barrel

1 *If you want to neaten things up a bit at this stage you can trim off more of the liner. The weight of the water will have pushed the liner into its final position.*

2 *Now begin to add the plants. Since they will be immersed in water, you can choose from a wide range of marginal plants that thrive in these conditions. Pot them into the plastic mesh baskets that you use for the pond.*

Here we show how to plant up the barrel prepared on pages 132-133. Of course, all kinds of troughs, pots, tubs and barrels are suitable for planting up in this way. Just make sure that they are painted inside with a sealant or lined with butyl rubber or plastic pond liner to ensure that they are watertight. Do remember that once filled with water, a few plants and any other water features you may chose, such as an ornament or fountain, the tub or pot is going to be extremely heavy, so decide on its final position while it is empty and plant it up in situ. If you are going to have to move the feature, place the container on a low platform with lockable casters for mobility. A water feature in a tub makes an excellent focal point for a dull corner of the garden or patio, where it might be raised on such a platform or a few bricks for extra prominence. Alternatively, stand it on a bed of pebbles or gravel or surround it with large stones and pots of lush plants to reinforce the watery effect. To show the tub at its best, make sure you position it against a suitable backdrop, such as a wall, fence or plain greenery. Large pebbles or a wall behind are also useful for installing concealed spouts for moving water effects to enhance the feature.

Smooth stones or boulders look best in small pools.

3 *If the display has a definite front view, then plan the planting with this in mind. Adding this low growing water forget-me-not towards the front will work well with the tall water buttercup at the back of the barrel.*

4 Once the planting is complete, you can add more stones to fill in spaces that seem to 'appear'. Adding another boulder here creates a better display. Be careful not to dislodge the outlet pipe of the pump as you move heavy items around.

5 Add cobbles and pebbles to match the color range and shape of the boulders. This helps the feature to look more like the bank of a natural stream. By now the barrel is very heavy and you should be working on it in its final location in the garden setting.

Lysimachia thyrsiflora

Ranunculus flammula

Iris versicolor 'Blue Light'

6 This is the final display with a three-tier spray fountain head fitted to the pump. The edges of the liner have been trimmed neatly around the top of the barrel.

Myosotis palustris

Epimedium x youngianum 'Roseum' (Not a marginal but would look attractive close to the barrel.)

Primula veris (Not suitable for inside the barrel, but this bog garden plant thrives in damp soil.)

7 If you prefer a bell-shaped effect then fit the appropriate head. Be careful not to pull out the central tube of the pump when changing heads.

Part Four
CREATIVE CONTAINERS

Using pots, tubs and troughs in the garden, you can grow what you like, where you like. You can move containers of plants around in much the same way as you might rearrange the furniture indoors and, what is more, you can even take them with you when you move house. Containers provide instant effect in the garden, as you can plant them up with a tremendous variety of shrubs, perennials, climbers, rock plants and annuals while the plants are in flower. Use containers to create pools of color on the patio, by the front or back door, by a seat, or wherever you need them all round the garden.

Containers are available in a wide range of materials and an even larger range of styles. There is no reason why you should not use a mixture of different types of containers all round the garden, although if you are making a group in a distinct area, such as the patio, it generally looks best to keep to one kind so they look like a 'set'. Some people choose containers to match the style of their house, garden or planting scheme. Others recycle 'finds', such as old baskets, or make their own 'one-off' containers. When it comes to choosing plants for containers, you might suppose that any plants sold in pots will grow in containers long-term, but this is not always the case. Some plants only tolerate containers when young, while naturally large trees and shrubs soon become potbound. But that still leaves the vast majority of plants as potential candidates, from traditional bedding plants, newly fashionable half-hardy annuals, low-maintenance mini-shrubs, grasses, alpines and heathers - and much more. You will find plenty of ideas on the following pages.

Left: *Flowers and vegetables flourish in a wooden trough.*   **Right:** *An oak barrel hosts a dwarf rhododendron.*

Choosing containers

Concrete tubs are long-lasting and generally quite frost-resistant, which makes them ideal for all-year-round plantings. Keep the outside clean by scrubbing with a stiff brush when necessary.

Good-quality plastic and other synthetic containers are long-lasting, resistant to cracking in winter and easy to wipe clean. Cheap plastics discolor, become brittle in sunlight and soon need replacing.

Traditional wire hanging baskets need lining before they can hold a planting mixture. Water them daily in summer - if they dry out, they are difficult to rewet. Plant the sides and base, as well as the top, for a stunning result.

Wooden containers have a natural look and are available as tubs, troughs or half-barrels. To prevent them rotting, treat the wood with timber preservative and line the inside with plastic.

Oriental-style glazed pots are good value - often far cheaper than similar terracotta pots. They are claimed to be frost resistant, so shouldn't crack if left outdoors in winter. They often come with matching saucers.

Fiber containers have a peatlike texture, but are actually made from recycled paper. They are cheap to buy, but slowly biodegrade as the material eventually absorbs water from the potting mixture inside.

Terracotta pots have a summery feel, but being porous, dry out much faster in summer than glazed or non-porous ones. Normal clay pots can crack if left outside in winter. Look for frost-proof terracotta.

This reproduction 'hayrack' is treated like half a hanging basket fixed to the wall. Line it with plastic or a liner designed for this type of container and plant through the sides, base and top for a brilliant display.

Modern solid-sided hanging baskets do not dry out as quickly as the traditional wire ones and do not need lining, but you can only plant the top. They are available as both round baskets to hang up and half baskets to go on a wall.

Crocking and liner options

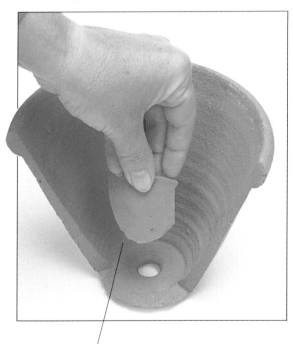

Above: *Woodlice, earthworms and slugs can get into pots through the drainage holes. To prevent this, cover the holes with plastic or the fine metal mesh sold for car bodywork repairs.*

Flowerpots come in two basic types: clay and plastic. Clay pots are porous, so the potting mixture in them dries out quickly due to evaporation through the sides. They are much heavier than plastics and the central drainage hole must be covered with a crock to prevent the soil washing away. Being lighter, plastic pots are the natural choice for roof gardens, hanging baskets and some windowboxes and wall pots. The potting mixture in them is slower to dry out as the sides of the pot are impervious to water, so take care when watering in dull conditions or when the plants are young or sickly and are using less water than usual. Plastic pots are easier to clean and take up less storage space, as they fit tightly inside one another.

Traditional wire hanging baskets must be lined before use. Moss-lined baskets look spectacular, as the wire framework allows you to plant the sides and base of the basket as well as the top, but they drip when watered and dry out quickly. Modern, solid-sided hanging baskets are easier to look after, but you cannot plant the sides. For the best of both worlds, use one of the modern liners inside a traditional basket.

Plastic pots usually have a ring of small drainage holes round the base.

Pieces from broken clay pots are known as 'crocks'.

Above: *Place a large piece of broken clay flowerpot, curved side up, over the drainage hole. Recycle broken clay pots by smashing them with a hammer.*

Clay pots have porous walls.

Plastic pots have thin impervious walls.

Above: *Clay containers have large holes in the base that need covering with crocks to keep the soil in, but allow surplus water to drain out.*

Above: *Plastic pots do not need crocking as soil is unlikely to escape through them, especially the coarser textured peaty potting mixtures.*

Crocking and liner options

Black plastic liners that you cut to shape are disposable and hold water well, but are not very attractive. Cut holes to plant the sides of the basket and make sure that plants soon cover the container.

Reusable coco-fiber looks natural and can be cut to fit. The overlapping panels allow you to plant around the sides of the basket.

Wire baskets must be lined before they will hold soil and plants; they are reusable for many years. Plastic-covered wire frames last longest.

Foam liners hold water well, can be cut to fit and are reusable. The overlapping flanges allow you to push plants through the sides of the basket. Choose natural colors.

Biodegradable, rigid liners are made of a compressed paperlike substance, colored and textured to resemble peat; they hold water well, but you cannot plant through the sides. They rarely last more than a year.

Sphagnum moss in bags is sold especially for lining baskets. It looks very good, but needs a great deal of watering.

Flexible liners with fitted bases are designed for baskets with a particular base size. You can trim them to fit baskets of different heights. Most kinds are reusable.

141

Choosing soils

Visit any garden center, and you will find a wide range of soils, grits, gravels, sands and chippings on sale. What to buy depends very much on what you plan to grow. The basic requirement is for a potting mixture. As a rule, a soil-based potting mixture is preferred for plants that are to be left in the same containers for more than one year, such as alpines and shrubs. This is because soil acts as a 'buffer' and holds more trace elements than peat products. A peat- or coir-based mixture is often preferred for annuals and other bedding plants or bulbs that will only remain in the containers for one growing season. They tend to retain water more than soil-based mixtures, which dry out faster. Plants in a peat or peat substitute mixture will need feeding after four to six weeks.

Right: Use ordinary potting mixture or a special hanging basket formula for hanging baskets and wall pots. If you choose an ordinary mix, peat or coir are usually preferable, as they are lighter in weight.

Ericaceous mix

Hanging basket mix

Above: A soil-based potting mixture is commonly used for plants that will be left in the same container for several years. Being heavier than peaty mixtures, containers that will be left outside in winter are more likely to remain upright in windy weather.

Soil-based potting mixture

Peat-based, multipurpose mix

Coir-based mix

142

Right: Horticultural, or potting, grit adds weight and air spaces to ordinary potting mixtures. It makes a good growing medium for plants that need particularly well-drained conditions.

Potting grit should contain a mixture of particle sizes, from fine sand to fine grit. Mix one part of grit to four of potting mixture.

Above: Place a layer of coarse grit over the crocks in a trough for herbs or alpines, which need good drainage. Use grit in the base of pots with bulbs left outside through the winter; bulbs will rot if left in wet soil.

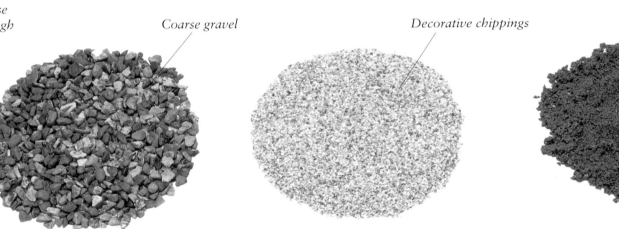

Coarse gravel

Decorative chippings

Potting grit

Left: Soil and peat-based potting mixes are the most commonly used. Use ericaceous mix for lime-hating plants. Coir is a 'green' alternative to peat. Hanging basket mixes usually contain water-retaining ingredients.

Right: Grit, chippings and mulching materials are useful optional extras, which can be used for improving drainage in potting mixtures or decorating the surface for certain types of plants grown in containers.

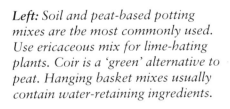

Cocoa shell

Bark chippings

Watering and feeding techniques

The secret of successful containers lies in regular feeding and watering. To flower well over a long season, plants need a continuous supply of nutrients - if they go short, the flowering quickly suffers. Check containers daily and water them whenever the potting mix feels dry. In a hot summer, well-filled containers in full bloom may need watering twice a day. Hanging baskets pose the biggest problems. Being high up, you cannot always reach them easily to water. When you do, they drip all over you, and if they dry out badly the water just bounces off the surface without soaking in. Fortunately, there are various products and devices to help with these problems. If you forget to feed regularly, use slow-release fertilizer pills, granules or sachets. If watering is a problem, try self-watering pots or add a water-retaining gel to the soil before planting. If you have several awkward baskets to water, it might be worth investing in a long-handled, hooked, hanging basket watering attachment for your hosepipe, or a device to raise and lower your baskets - buy one for each basket.

Slow-release fertilizer granules

You can mix slow-release fertilizer granules with the potting mixture before planting up a container. To 'top up' later in the season, simply sprinkle more granules over the soil or make a hole with a pencil and push the granules into it. Alternatively, you can buy small bags containing a measured dose of granules. Always read the manufacturer's instructions carefully to see how long you can expect slow-release feeds to last, as individual products vary.

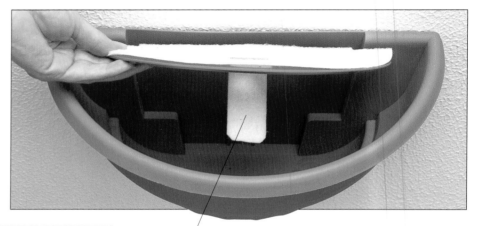

As the soil dries out, the wick draws up water.

Above: *This wall basket has a water reservoir built into the base. It stores any surplus water that drains through from the soil above until it is needed.*

Water-retaining gel

Mix the dry granules with water and stir to make a thick gel. Combine with the potting mixture. The gel crystals soak up surplus water for later release as the soil dries out.

Right: *Terracotta 'water wells' such as this have a wide neck with a spike-shaped base below that is easy to push into the potting mix. Water seeps slowly out through the porous sides so that the soil can absorb it gradually.*

Above: Press slow-release fertilizers 'pills' firmly into middle of the soil. The nutrients will slowly escape whenever the potting mix is moist.

Below: Make a watering funnel by cutting a plastic bottle in half. Remove the stopper. Push the neck into the soil so that the funnel is half buried.

Below: When the funnel is filled, the soil wedged in the neck prevents the water running out too quickly. This method is ideal for hanging baskets.

Above: To lower the basket, release the brake by lifting the basket from below. Support the basket with one hand and let it drop quite quickly. To engage the brake, let the basket slow down as it approaches the right height.

Above: Hose attachments for watering hanging baskets have an on/off switch on the handle, so you only need squirt once the business end is in position. They are invaluable if you have a lot of high baskets.

Below: Water the basket and then raise it back to its original height with a hand supporting it underneath as before. Check that the brake has engaged again before releasing the basket.

Making a container from hypertufa

The outer box will be the depth of the finished container.

1 *Select two strong cardboard boxes that fit one inside the other, leaving a gap between them of about 2in(5cm) all round.*

2 *Cut a piece of board to fit exactly inside the base of the larger, outer box. Nail four wine corks as shown - these will eventually form the drainage holes in the base of the finished container.*

Cement powder

Genuine old stone containers, such as butlers' sinks, are highly sought after by collectors for growing alpines and are very expensive. But there is an alternative; you can now make your own containers from a fake stone mixture called hypertufa. The ingredients are available from any garden center or hardware store. It is cheap, and very versatile. You can cover an old ceramic sink, provided the shiny surface of the sink is first given a coating of outdoor-quality building adhesive. This gives it a rough surface to which the hypertufa can 'key in', otherwise the mixture just slides off. Hypertufa can transform an old container, such as a clay flowerpot, into a stone one, just by giving it a new outer finish. If you have large terracotta pots that have cracked, a coating of hypertufa can hide a repair, where the broken pieces have been joined by a suitable adhesive. You can also make your own free-style containers from scratch using the mixture to cover a foundation made of scrunched up small-mesh chicken wire. Or you could try the cardboard box method, shown here, to make a 'stone' sink or trough.

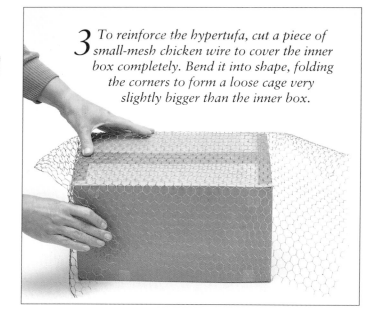

3 *To reinforce the hypertufa, cut a piece of small-mesh chicken wire to cover the inner box completely. Bend it into shape, folding the corners to form a loose cage very slightly bigger than the inner box.*

4 *Slip the smaller box with its wire cover into the larger box. If the wire sticks out at all, bend it down more firmly until it slips in easily.*

5 To make hypertufa, mix equal parts by volume of cement, gritty sand and moss peat or coconut fiber-based peat substitute with enough water to mix to a sloppy paste.

Peat or coir-based substitute

Coarse gritty sand

6 Remove the inner box and wire netting, and trowel enough of the hypertufa mixture over the board base to come to the top of the corks. Do not cover them.

7 Fit the inner box and wire cover into the center and press down firmly, so the wire sinks into the hypertufa and the gap between the boxes is even all round. Fill the gap with hypertufa.

Covering a flowerpot with hypertufa

Start by soaking the flowerpot in water. This is particularly important if you are using a brand new pot. Then, using rubber gloves, press handfuls of the hypertufa all over the surface and stand the pot in a sheltered place to dry slowly. The coarse sand and peat in the mixture will give the pot a rough stonelike texture.

Cover the inside rim of the pot so that when it is planted, the original clay surface will not be visible.

8 Use a piece of wood to ram the mixture well down between the two boxes on each side of the wire mesh so that there are no air pockets. These would turn out as holes in the sides of the finished container.

9 Finish off by roughly rounding and smoothing the exposed surface of the hypertufa - this will form the edges of the container.

Do not worry if the sides of the outer box bow out slightly, this will only improve the finished shape.

The container emerges

Hypertufa takes a long time to dry out, so make the container where you will not need to move it, or put it on top of a firm wooden base that you can lift without touching the sides of the container. Allow six weeks for a large sink or trough made by the cardboard box method to set before you remove the boxes. Do not worry if there are some imperfections, as they add character. Any air pockets left while the hypertufa was in the mold will be apparent as holes in the sides of the container. If they go right through, or can be enlarged to do so, transform them into side planting pockets. Hypertufa continues to dry for a time after the mold is removed. When it is completely dry it turns a pale gray color very similar to stone. If you used coarse textured sand and peat in the mix, it will also have a craggy texture. The longer you leave hypertufa containers outside in the open air, the more weathered and stonelike they become. To speed up the aging process, spray the sides with diluted liquid houseplant feed. This encourages lichens and moss to gradually colonize them, creating the look of a genuine aged stone container.

3 Carefully cut away the cardboard from the sides of the container. Do not hurry or you may pull pieces of hypertufa away with the cardboard. Peel off loose paper shreds with your fingers.

2 Remove the inner box by folding it inwards, then lifting out the base one end at a time. Take your time, as forcing it may damage the container.

1 After six weeks, gently peel back the sides of the inner cardboard box to check if the hypertufa is 'done'. Even so, it will not be very firm, so treat it gently for several more weeks.

4 You can sometimes remove thin slivers of paper on the sides of the container by wetting them and then peeling them off with a knife, or by wire-brushing. They will eventually disappear when the trough has been out in the garden for a while.

A drop of liquid detergent in the water helps to remove scraps of cardboard sticking to the surface.

Use the wire brush to roughen up smooth surfaces.

5 Gently turn the container over to remove the cardboard from the base. Prise the wooden board away from the base. The corks will be left behind in the hypertufa.

6 Drill through the corks to make the drainage holes in the base of the container. This is much safer than trying to drill holes into the hypertufa, which could crumble and split.

7 The finished container is ready for planting, with a sensible number of drainage holes for its size - something genuine old sinks never have. When it is standing in its final position, raise the container on two bricks to allow surplus water to drain away.

Round off any sharp edges with a wire brush.

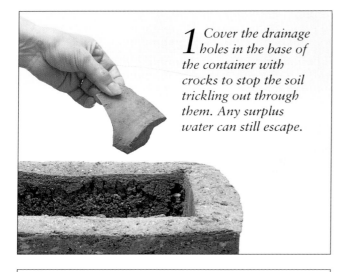

1 Cover the drainage holes in the base of the container with crocks to stop the soil trickling out through them. Any surplus water can still escape.

2 Whatever soil you use, put a 1-2in(2.5-5cm) layer of coarse gravel over the base to assist drainage and stop crocks becoming clogged.

Alpines in hypertufa

Any plants that will grow in normal containers will also grow in hypertufa, but stone or hypertufa containers are mostly used for rock plants. All sorts of alpines, dwarf bulbs and drought-tolerant small shrubs are suitable, as long as you only group together plants that share similar soil conditions and cultural requirements. Plants that need particularly well-drained potting mix, such as encrusted saxifrages, armerias, erodiums, sedums, sempervivums and lewisias, do best in a mixture of 1 part grit to 4 parts soil-based potting mix. Less fussy rock plants, such as arabis, aubretia, diascia, small hardy cranesbills, such as *Geranium lancastriense,* and most campanulas are quite happy in soil-based potting mix on its own. Gentians can be grown in containers, but need relatively moisture-retentive soil as they dislike drying out; a half-and-half mixture of peat and soil-based potting soils with a little added grit would be best. (Check plant care labels with gentians as some varieties only grow in lime-free soil). They also like partial shade. In a very shady spot, fill the container with the peat/soil mix and plant ramonda and haberlea or primula species and small hardy ferns, such as *Adiantum pedatum,* the bird's foot fern, and *Adiantum venustum,* the hardy maidenhair fern. They all need rather damper conditions than normal alpines; the soil should never quite dry out. Larger shrubby rock plants for stone or fake stone containers include helianthemum, cistus and hebes: the whipcord hebes have dramatic stringlike foliage, although others have more striking flowers.

Fill the container almost to the rim.

3 For growing alpines in this container, add 1 part of coarse grit to 4 parts of soil-based potting mixture.

Coarse grit

Soil-based potting mix

4 To create an authentic alpine look, bury a craggy chunk of tufa rock in the center of the container as though it were a natural outcrop.

5 This trough has a small hole where an air pocket was left in the mixture. It makes a planting hole for a sedum, pushed through from outside.

6 Choose alpines that need the same soil and growing conditions. Flowering kinds and those with hillocky shapes and colored foliage make interesting combinations.

7 Evergreen plants look interesting in winter when many alpines die down to ground level. In time, they will creep over the sides of the trough and up the tufa chunk.

Hebe in a hypertufa pot

The hypertufa-covered pot made at the same time as the trough has dried to a stonelike color and would look good standing next to it planted with a compact rockery type shrub. The Hebe franciscana shown here teams well with the rock plants in the trough. Once you have planted the pot, you can also spray the sides with a diluted houseplant feed so that moss and lichen develop to make it look old.

8 Topdress the finished surface with coarse grit, such as granite chippings. It helps to improve surface drainage and prevents alpines rotting at the neck.

9 The planted container already begins to look like real stone. You can spray the sides with dilute liquid feed to encourage mosses and lichens to grow.

Campanula muralis

Sempervivum *hybrid*

Saxifraga correovensis

Erodium 'Natasha'

Sedum spurium 'Variegatum'

Rhodohypoxis 'Fred Broome'

Sedum 'Lydium'

A versatile windowbox

Windowboxes are on show all the time and so the whole display can be spoiled if one plant is past its best. In this case, it pays to leave plants in their pots and just 'plunge' them into the container up to their rims. You can then lift out and replace individual plants without disturbing the others, leaving a wreath of foliage such as trailing ivy round the edge and altering the flowers in between them as the seasons change. You might choose spring bulbs and polyanthus for instant color in spring, replacing them with annuals, pelargoniums or fuchsias, or perhaps a mixture of culinary and flowering herbs for the summer. In autumn and winter, big cities create their own mild microclimate, allowing you to plant cool-temperature indoor plants, such as cyclamen and exacum, in windowboxes out of doors. (Do not try this unless you have seen other people in your area use the strategy successfully.) It is worth leaving foliage plants in their pots too, so that they can be easily replaced if necessary. As well as ivies, small upright conifer trees and many houseplants (such as asparagus fern) can be used as temporary foliage plants for windowboxes. To look after a windowbox display like this, feed and water the plants regularly. Check the potting mix daily in summer and in windy weather, when they are liable to dry out more rapidly. And keep the soil around the pots moist; as well as helping to keep the plants watered, this creates a humid pocket of air around the plants, which they enjoy.

3 Place the plants, in their pots, into the box. In this formal, symmetrical display, trails of ivy cascade over the sides and flowering plants are grouped in the center.

This Swan River daisy will form the central part of the arrangement.

1 This wooden windowbox has its own rigid plastic liner. It prevents the wood being in contact with damp soil, which could cause the wood to rot. There are no drainage holes.

2 Arrange the plants in front of the windowbox. Place 1in(2.5cm) of soilless potting mix in the plastic liner and make a small depression for each pot to stand in.

Ringing the changes

Here, just the Brachycome and two of the ageratums have been lifted out of the middle of the display and replaced with a tuberous-rooted begonia to show the effect that a small change has on the arrangement.

4 Fill the space between the pots with more potting mix. This helps to keep the pots in place and retains moisture, acting as a reserve from which the plants can draw as needed.

5 It is easy to lift out fading plants and replace them with fresh ones. Experiment with new 'looks' or alter the composition for a change.

Ageratum

Pelargonium

Swan River daisy (Brachycome)

Trailing ivy

Planting up a wooden barrel

Wooden half barrels are the favorite choice for permanently planting woodland shrubs, such as dwarf rhododendron, pieris or camellia, as they go so well together. You will need a large barrel, but do not choose one larger than you can comfortably move when it is full of soil. A 12in(30cm) container is the very smallest you should consider; 15-18in(38-45cm) is better and 24in(60cm) the ultimate. The larger the container, the larger the plant will be able to grow, because there will be more room for the roots. In a small pot the plant will be naturally dwarfed, but it will also dry out very quickly and need more frequent watering.

The rhododendron featured here is a lime-hating plant that needs to be planted in a lime-free potting mixture and not the normal kind. Special lime-free (ericaceous) potting mixtures are available, but these do not normally contain soil, being based on peat or coir instead. On their own, they are not ideal for plants that will be left in the same container for several years. You can make up your own mixture, consisting of half ericaceous soil and half soil-based potting material. There is a little lime in this, but the mixture seems to suit ericaceous plants. If you prefer to plant other shrubs, choose reasonably compact kinds and fill the container with normal soil-based potting mix.

1 Allow the plastic sheet to hang over the sides of the barrel. Partly fill the barrel with a mixture of ericaceous and soil-based potting mix.

Treating a wooden barrel

1 Drill a hole at least 0.5in(1.25cm) in diameter in the base of the barrel. Alternatively, you could make a group of smaller holes.

2 A drainage hole is essential, especially for plants left outdoors in winter, otherwise the potting mix becomes waterlogged in wet weather.

3 Paint the barrel inside and out (including the base) with plant-friendly wood preservative. To allow any paint fumes to disappear, leave the barrel to dry out completely for a few days before proceeding.

4 Take a square of unperforated plastic at least four times as wide as the barrel, lay it over the top and push the middle down to form a loose lining. Push the center 2in(5cm) out through the hole in the base.

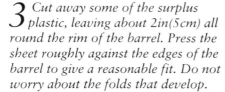

4 Roll back the remaining plastic and tuck it neatly inside the edge of the barrel so that it does not show. In this way, the plastic becomes a 'collar' that prevents the compost touching the wood. Again, this is to prevent the risk of rotting the wood.

2 Knock the plant out of its pot and place it in the center of the barrel. If the pot is filled with roots, gently tease a few of them out first, otherwise they will not be able to grow out into the compost.

3 Cut away some of the surplus plastic, leaving about 2in(5cm) all round the rim of the barrel. Press the sheet roughly against the edges of the barrel to give a reasonable fit. Do not worry about the folds that develop.

5 Cut the tip off the plastic sheet protruding through the hole in the base of the barrel. This allows the excess water to drain away from the potting soil without wetting the wood and thus reduces the risk of rotting.

5 Fill round the roots with more potting mix, leaving the top of the rootball level with the surface. The plant should be no deeper in the barrel than it was in the original pot.

Leave 1in(2.5cm) between the soil surface and the rim of the barrel for watering.

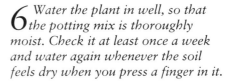

6 Water the plant in well, so that the potting mix is thoroughly moist. Check it at least once a week and water again whenever the soil feels dry when you press a finger in it.

A pot for a shady place

Since most of the plants traditionally grown in containers are sun-lovers, shady areas can be some of the most difficult to 'decorate' with pots. However, many plants that are suitable for shady gardens grow well in containers. Hydrangeas and clumps of hostas make good specimen plants to grow on their own in large pots. Small plants make more of a show when grouped together in large containers. All the plants featured here are moisture lovers, so select a container that retains moisture well and looks at home in moist shady conditions. The one shown here is a fiber pot, made from recycled paper. This type of container will biodegrade after a few years in the garden, but is not expensive to buy. Good plants for growing in containers in shade include lady's mantle (*Alchemilla mollis*), *Ajuga* (ornamental bugle, which has colored leaves and blue flowers), cultivated celandines, *Pulmonaria* (lungwort), which has silver spotted leaves, *Brunnera* (perennial forget-me-not), plus camellia, miniature rhododendrons and pieris. Few annuals will tolerate shade for more than half a day, but *Impatiens* (busy lizzie) will thrive if they are already flowering when you plant them.

4 Plant the foliage plant first - here a hardy fern - and add the flowering plants next. Knock each one carefully out of its pot and plant it without breaking up the ball of roots.

3 Choose the plants and, leaving them in their pots for the time being, stand them together in the container while you decide which ones look best next to each other.

1 Large fiber pots may have several holes around the sides of the base, rather than one large one in the middle, as you find with many containers. Cover each hole with a 'crock' to keep the compost in.

2 Fill the pot to within 2in(5cm) of its rim with soil-based potting mixture. This will suit the perennials to be planted here, as they will remain in the container for several years and its weight keeps the pot stable.

5 Finish off by tucking a few trailing plants, such as the ivies used here, around the sides to soften the edge of the container. Alternative edging plants for shade include Ajuga *(bugle)* and Alchemilla mollis *(lady's mantle)*.

6 Trickle a few handfuls of potting mixture between the plants to fill any gaps and leave the surface level. Check that the plants are left growing at the same depth as they were when planted in their original pots.

7 As a finishing touch, twist the trails of ivy together to form a definite edge to the planting, instead of letting them dangle over the sides. Hold the ends in place with 'twist ties' (paper-covered wire).

Hardy fern
(Dryopteris filix-mas
'Crispula Crispata')

Drumstick primula
(Primula denticulata)

Ivy
(Hedera helix)

Primrose
(Primula
vulgaris)

Viola
labradorica

Planting up a plastic urn

A formal container such as an urn looks best teamed with a similarly formal style of planting. The traditional scheme shown here uses a tall foliage plant in the middle of the urn, with smaller flowering ones around the edge. It could stand in the middle of a small formal courtyard garden or patio, or on a corner or next to a doorway where it looks good from every angle. The upright conifer in the center adds to the feeling of formality because of its shape. The same plant could be left permanently as a centerpiece, while several changes of annuals are planted around it in successive springs and summers. When it grows too big for the urn or its roots take up all the space so that there is no room to plant anything else, it can be replaced. When this happens, perhaps after two years, you can put the original plant in the garden or feature it as a specimen plant in a big pot. Alternatively, you could make a temporary display by plunging all the plants in their pots up to their rims in the urn and lifting them out as they finish flowering or when you fancy a change of plants.

1 Drill a drainage hole if there is not one already there. Most plastic containers have positions marked where the plastic is thinner to make drilling easier.

2 Cover the drainage hole with a 'crock' - a concave piece of broken flowerpot. This is to stop the potting mix running out through the hole when you water.

4 Loosely fill the container with potting mixture to within 2in(5cm) of the rim. A soilless one will be quite suitable for the conifer and annuals to be planted in this container.

3 Add a trowelful of grit to the bottom of the container to provide extra drainage and prevent the soil being washed out under the crock. Use potting grit, which is a fine grade and ideal for this purpose.

If you are reusing a plastic container, first wash it out thoroughly and remove stuck-on roots. It should be as clean and smooth on the inside as on the outside.

5 *Start by planting up the center of the urn. Put the tallest plant here for a symmetrical display. This upright dwarf conifer is ideal.*

8 *Water the plants well in. As the container is well filled with plants, expect it to dry out quickly. Water it thoroughly every time it feels dry. Do not let the plants dry out and wilt or they will not flower so well.*

Chamaecyparis lawsoniana 'Ellwoodii'

Miniature marguerite Chrysanthemum 'Snow Lady'

Turk's turban (Ranunculus asiaticus)

Bedding tulip

Bellis perennis 'Goliath'

Ajuga 'Burgundy Glow'

Bellis perennis 'Pomponette'

6 *Plant the edge of the urn with flowering plants, such as the Ranunculus, bellis daisies, miniature marguerite and Ajuga. They contrast well with the foliage in the center.*

7 *When planting is complete, top up any hollows between the plants with enough potting mixture to fill the container to within 1in(2.5cm) of the rim and leave the surface level.*

Planting daffodils and anemones

With daffodils, tulips and hyacinths in containers, a patio can be a riot of color from early spring onwards. Dry bulbs are on sale in garden centers in the fall. Buy daffodils as soon as they are available and plant them straightaway, as they start rooting earlier than many spring bulbs. Choose compact bulb varieties, as tall-stemmed kinds may get broken by breezes eddying around a patio. The bulbs should be plump and healthy, without any cuts and bruises or moldy bits; the biggest bulbs will bear the most flowers. You can plant containers entirely with one kind of bulb, but if you want to mix them, choose bulbs that flower at roughly the same time. When it comes to planting, there is no need to use bulb fiber, which is intended for indoor use. Normal peat- or soil-based potting mixture is fine. After planting, stand the containers outdoors in a cool, shady spot protected from heavy rain. (Very often they will be fine in a shady part of the patio next to a wall, since the wall deflects most of the rain). When the first shoots appear, move the containers to their positions on the patio. While the bulbs are flowering, feed them weekly with general-purpose liquid feed. When they are over, tip them out and plant them in the garden. You can then reuse the container for a summer bedding scheme. Buy new bulbs for the following year's container display, as they will flower better than the old ones.

4 Press each bulb gently down into the potting mixture, giving it a half turn. This ensures that the base of the bulb makes good contact with the soil - essential for rooting.

1 If your container does not have drainage holes in the base, you should drill some. It is vital that containers that will be standing outdoors during the winter can drain freely.

2 Place 1-2in(2.5-5cm) of coarse gravel over the base of the container to aid drainage. Bulbs can easily rot if the potting mix is too wet.

3 Put 1-2in(2.5-5cm) of potting mixture over the gravel. Ideally, bulbs should be planted with twice their own depth of potting mix above the tip of the bulb, but this may not be possible in containers.

5 *The more bulbs you get in, the better the display will be. Put the bulbs as close together as you can, without allowing them to touch each other or the sides of the container.*

6 *Cover the bulbs with just enough potting mix to leave the tips on show so you can see where they are when you plant the second layer above.*

7 *Gently press in some more bulbs between the tips of the lower layer. A few Anemone blanda corms will make a contrast with the daffodils.*

Below: This cross section shows the layers of bulbs in the container, with the daffodils 'Golden Harvest' below and the Anemone blanda 'Blue Shade' dotted above them.

Right: The daffodil 'Golden Harvest' is a traditional variety once used for cut flower production but now a garden favorite. The daffodils will do best if the container is placed in the sun, but they tolerate light shade.

Right: Anemone blanda grows to 6in(15cm) and is usually available in mixed colors, although separate shades are sometimes sold. Blue is one of the most popular.

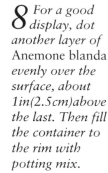

8 *For a good display, dot another layer of Anemone blanda evenly over the surface, about 1in(2.5cm)above the last. Then fill the container to the rim with potting mix.*

9 *Cover this layer of bulbs with a little more soil, leaving it roughly level on top. Take care not to knock over the bulbs, as they are still quite unstable.*

1 *Choose a deep trough; it is not vital to plant bulbs to twice their own depth, but try for it. Make plenty of drainage holes, as tulips need good drainage.*

Planting tulips in a container

Tulips are another good group of bulbs for containers. If your garden does not provide the conditions they need - well-drained soil and a warm sheltered spot - growing in containers is the best way of catering for them. There are lots of different types of tulips. The earliest to flower are waterlily tulips - the kaufmanniana and fosterii hybrids. These are neat compact plants, with sturdy flowers that open out wide like waterlilies in the sun. They flower at early daffodil time. Greigii hybrid tulips look very similar, but have vividly variegated leaves, dappled with red or purplish splotches, that contrast well with the brightly colored flowers. They flower a few weeks later. These are all compact and ideal for containers. Team them with tubs of spring bedding plants, such as wallflowers, polyanthus, violas, forget-me-nots and bellis daisies for a dazzling display.

Most other tulips flower later, in early summer. These can also be grown in containers, but they need a well-sheltered spot, as their taller stems are very fragile. Tulips should be planted after daffodils, in mid-fall, to prevent the bulbs rotting - they start rooting later. Feed and water the growing tulips as you would other bulbs in containers. After the flowers are over, tip the plants out and transplant them temporarily to some spare ground. When the leaves have died down naturally, dig up the bulbs and let them dry off completely. Twist off any dead foliage or stems, and store the dry bulbs in a cool, dry, dark place for the summer. The early-flowering hybrids mentioned above can then be replanted on a rockery in the garden; tall tulips need a well-drained flowerbed. Unlike many spring bulbs, tulips do best if they are dug up and stored dry for the summer as they easily rot if left in the ground.

2 *Put 1-2in(2.5-5cm) of coarse gravel in the bottom of the trough. This prevents the drainage holes from clogging with potting mix. There is no need to cover small holes with crocks. Smooth out the gravel to make it level.*

3 *Add 1-2in(2.5-5cm) of soil- or peat-based potting mix. You can use up any remaining mixture left over from summer.*

4 *Remove the dead, brown, outer skins from the tulip bulbs. This helps them to root well and removes any lingering disease spores that may be present on the old skin.*

5 *We are planting five different varieties in this trough, so we have decided to plant them in five groups of five rather than mixing them up. Press bulbs lightly down into the soil.*

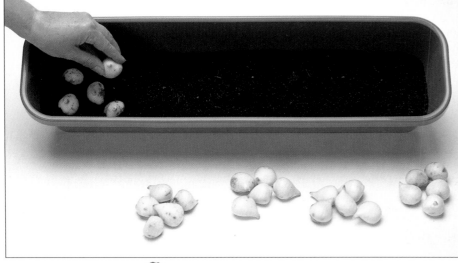

6 *Arrange the groups of bulbs so that there are small gaps between each group. You can then tuck forget-me-not plants in between the bulbs early next spring. They 'go' very nicely with tulips.*

7 *When all the bulbs are planted, cover them with potting mixture, taking care not to knock them over. Fill the container with more soil to within 0.5in(1.25cm) of the rim .*

Below: *These healthy tulip bulbs have been cleaned of their dead, outer skins and planted in a trough. This planting depth is fine for this container.*

8 *Water the soil all over so that it is uniformly moist, but not saturated. Tulips rot easily if kept too damp. Stand the trough in a sheltered spot.*

Left: *'Red Riding Hood' is one of the Greigii hybrids (peacock tulips) whose flowers open in the sun to show their centers. The leaves of this variety are mottled with dark purple streaks.*

A plastic tub of annuals

Plastic containers are a bit different to work with than some materials. Plastic is not porous, so the compost in it does not dry out so quickly. This is a benefit on hot summer days, but can be a problem at the start of the season, as small, young plants do not use a great deal of water, especially when the weather is cool. It is easy to overwater them, especially if you use a peat-based potting mixture, which holds much more water than other types. Water with care for the first four to five weeks. Another difference lies in the drainage holes. Plastic pots usually have several holes spread around the base. Because the holes are quite small, there is no need to cover them with crocks, especially if you use a soilless potting mixture, which is more fibrous in texture and less likely to trickle out. Some plastic containers are dual purpose so they do not have drainage holes ready made. You can use the pot without holes, for example, when the container is to stand on a floor that you do not want to be marked by water. If you do want holes in the base, knock through the weak points marked, with the tip of a screwdriver. Some people prefer plastic containers for plants that only last one season - typically spring or summer annuals. This is probably a throwback to the days when plastic containers were rather poor quality and often became brittle after a year or two out in the sunlight. A hard frost in winter was often enough to make them disintegrate entirely. But nowadays, good-quality plastics are available that last very much better and can be used outside all year round.

1 *This container is to be planted with a selection of annual flowers, so choose a soilless potting mixture and fill it to just below the rim.*

2 *Group a selection of plants to see how they look together. This is a bright color scheme of red, yellow and orange. As one of them is a climber, place a cane in the middle of the tub to support it.*

3 *Plant the center-piece first - here a climbing black-eyed Susan. Tie it loosely to the cane and tie in new stems regularly.*

5 *A foliage plant makes a good 'foil' for groups of flowers. This coleus goes very well with the color scheme of the container.*

7 *Water the finished container well. It should look well filled with plants; as they grow, the effect will become even more abundant-looking. Once the container is filled with roots, water it once or twice a day.*

6 *The cream and green variegated ornamental cabbage will eventually make a huge rosette shape at the base of the container. By then, the other flowers will have grown quite tall.*

4 *Arrange the other plants in groups of the same type, next to neighbors that make a strong contrast, with flowers of different sizes, colors and shapes.*

Black-eyed Susan
(Thunbergia alata)

Argyranthemum frutescens
'Jamaica Primrose'

African marigold,
compact type

Ornamental
cabbage

Salvia
'Vanguard'

Coleus

French
marigold
'Aurora Fire'

Planting a large traditional hanging basket

Traditional hanging baskets are made of an open latticework of wire. This makes it possible to plant not only the top, but the sides and base of the basket as well, to create a perfect ball of bloom. Wire baskets must be lined before they can hold any potting mix. Although you could use any of the basket liners available in garden centers, or even black plastic, live moss is the traditional choice and certainly looks best. Sphagnum moss is sold ready-bagged in garden centers for this purpose. If possible, take a look at it first and choose fresh, green, live moss, which makes an attractive background for basket plants. Moss that has been allowed to dry out and turn brown will not green up again later. Some people recommend raking moss out of the lawn to use in hanging baskets. Although it looks green to start with, moss obtained this way quickly goes brown after the basket has been planted. If you are planting a traditional hanging basket, it is a good idea to stick to a traditional type of planting scheme. This basically involves using a mixture of plants - trailers, upright and even sometimes small climbers - in a wide range of colors. Traditional favorites include the plants shown in this attractive arrangement - ivy-leaved pelargoniums (the trailing kind, often referred to as geraniums), petunias, trailing lobelias, and both trailing and upright fuchsias. Other annual bedding plants are often used, too - French marigolds and busy lizzie, for instance - while tuberous begonias, available as both upright and trailing varieties, are also good choices.

5 Lay a second tier of trailing plants (in this case more lobelia), so that they rest between the first row of plants and a few inches above them.

1 *Traditional wire baskets have a rounded base, so sit them in a bucket to hold them firmly while you plant them up. Line the bottom with tight wads of moss for a firm base.*

2 *Trailing lobelia is suitable for the sides and base of the basket. Press the plants carefully out of their trays with a finger or the tip of a pencil or cane to avoid damaging the roots.*

3 *Lay the plants on their sides, with their roots on the mossy base and the stems hanging out from the lower edge of the basket. Add a little soil to hold the roots in place if you wish.*

4 *Add another layer of moss to the edge of the basket until about half the sides are covered. Dense wads of moss will retain the soil more effectively than loose fluffy strands.*

Planting a large traditional hanging basket

Ivy leaved geranium 'Amethyst'

Upright fuchsia 'Beacon Rosa'

Purple petunia

Petunia 'Pink vein'

6 Continue adding moss right up to the rim or slightly above it. Add soilless potting mixture to the center of the basket, filling the gaps around the rootballs of the plants that have already been put in.

Verbena 'Carousel'

Lobelia 'Fountain'

Trailing fuchsia 'Frank Saunders'

7 Plant the top of the basket with a mixture of upright and trailing plants. Knock them out of their pots first and plant them closely together so the basket looks full from the start.

8 Lift the chains carefully to avoid damaging the plants. Hang the basket in a sheltered sunny place. Water it well in, and water daily to prevent the soil drying out.

Using a rigid liner

Superb though they undoubtedly look, traditional wire hanging baskets suffer from one major drawback. If you line them with moss, they dry out quickly and are very difficult to rewet. If you do not favor a plastic, solid-sided hanging basket, one solution is to try a different liner. Fiber liners, made of recycled paper, resemble compressed peat, but the liner is far less porous than moss. The fiber sides soak up water, which helps to keep the compost moist. Unless the basket is heavily overwatered, it won't drip as much as moss-lined baskets tend to do. The one disadvantage of preformed fiber liners is that you cannot plant through the sides and base. If you cut holes in the liner, you run the risk of compost washing out, as well as water dripping, so it is better not to do so. Even so, by planting plenty of trailing plants at both the sides and top of the basket, you can still achieve a very pretty, traditional-looking basket, without the hard work associated with moss. To achieve a 'ball of bloom look', space out the stems of trailing plants around the basket and tie them down onto the wire frame. This stops the ends of the shoots turning up towards the light and encourages them to branch out, which gives the basket a better covering. As with any hanging basket, check the potting mix at least once a day and water it well as soon as it begins to feel dry - or even slightly before. If you did not add a slow-release fertilizer when the basket was planted, be sure to feed it regularly - at least once a week - with a good liquid or soluble feed to keep the plants flowering well. Nip off the dead flowerheads for the same reason.

3 Stand the basket on top of a bucket to hold it upright. The ivy-leaved pelargonium in the center stays reasonably upright if surrounded by other plants.

This fiber liner is made from recycled paper.

1 Choose the right size liner for your basket. It is a good idea to take the basket with you when buying the liner to be sure of obtaining a good fit.

2 Place the liner in the basket and fill it with potting mixture. Choose suitable plants and knock them out of their pots before planting them in the liner.

Soilless mixes are ideal for hanging baskets.

Ivy-leaved
geranium 'Beauty
of Eastbourne'

Lobelia 'Sapphire'

4 Finish off by tucking small
trailing lobelias into the gaps
between the larger plants. These
will cascade over
the sides, hiding
most of the liner
from view.

Miniature regal
pelargonium

Pink petunia

5 Lift the chains carefully over the
plants and hang up the finished
basket in its final position. Water it in
thoroughly. The basket will need this
good soaking to start with, as the fiber
liner absorbs a great deal of water.

1 Place a flexible liner inside the basket. Press it well down and overlap adjacent panels to achieve a good fit.

Using a flexible basket liner

Many types of natural and synthetic flexible liners are available for use with traditional wire hanging baskets. These offer the best possible compromise between moss and a rigid liner. Flexible liners are made from a series of panels that, when pushed down inside the basket, overlap slightly to take up the shape of the container. They can be made of foam plastic, coconut fiber or the rather less flexible 'whalehide'. The advantage of this type of liner is that, where the panels overlap, you are left with small slits through which you can put the plants. This makes it possible to create the spectacular 'ball of bloom', characteristic of a traditional moss-lined basket. However, because the liner is made of a more water-retentive material, the basket will not dry out or drip as much as a mossed one. As with a traditional moss-lined basket, it is good idea to place an old saucer or circle of plastic into the base of the basket after lining, which helps to stop the water dripping straight out through the bottom. When planting a traditional wire basket - which has a rounded base - stand it inside the top of a bucket for support. Start with the difficult areas - the sides - by planting as low down as you can, as this will give a better result. Then plant the top. Aim to pack as many plants into the basket as you can for maximum impact. If you think that the basket may be difficult to water once it is full, try a useful tip. Cut a few inches from the neck end of a plastic bottle and make a funnel (see page 145). Sink this into the middle of the basket, hidden between the plants, with just the top above soil level. Then, every time you water, fill the funnel and water will trickle down into the heart of the basket instead of running away down the sides.

2 Plant the sides by pushing the plant roots through the slits between the panels. Then tuck the edges of the panels firmly around the plants to prevent soil from leaking out.

3 Fill the basket to the rim with potting mixture, making sure it completely surrounds the roots of the plants that have already been put in.

4 Next, begin planting the top of the basket. These three bushy fuchsias will give some height among the other plants, which are predominantly trailing species.

5 *Plant an ivy-leaved pelargonium and petunias in the gaps between the fuchsias. Knock all the plants out of their pots first.*

Single red petunia

Ivy-leaved pelargonium 'Scarlet Galilee'

Fuchsia 'Meike Meursing'

6 *Firm each plant gently in, leaving a shallow depression around the inside edge of the basket to make watering easier. If the basket is overfilled, water bounces off the top.*

Helichrysum microphylla

Pink and red impatiens

7 *As a finishing touch, spread out the long shoots of fuchsia and other plants evenly around the sides of the basket and fix them to the wire framework using flexible plant ties.*

8 *Finally, gather up the chains, taking care not to damage the plants, and hang up the basket. Water it well, allowing the potting mixture to absorb some of the water before adding more, until it is moist through.*

171

Planting up a plastic wall planter

1 *If possible, stand the planter on its base while you are planting it. Some do not have a flat base and most are top heavy, so if this is difficult, hang it in its final position and fill it almost to the rim with potting mixture.*

Imagine a hanging basket sliced in half vertically through the middle, with the flat side stuck against a wall. That is a wall planter. Some wall planters are constructed very much like half hanging baskets, with a wire framework that needs lining in much the same way as a traditional hanging basket. If you choose this type, you will also need a liner for it. Special liners are made in a range of sizes to fit. However, unless you have plenty of time for watering, open-sided wall planters can be rather disappointing, as the plants in them dry out almost in front of your eyes. Wall planters with solid sides are generally more practical. Even so, they dry out quite quickly compared to containers at ground level. This is partly because the containers themselves are so much smaller and also because, being raised up, they are surrounded by breezes that cause water to evaporate from the soil faster than usual. Once you have taken these factors into account, wall planters can look most attractive. Being small, they are usually placed in a 'key' position where they are very visible, so be sure to use only the very best plants in them. Formal arrangements are probably the most suitable, but you could experiment with informal ones. These usually work best if you group a collection of planters in the same style at different levels on a wall. You will only need a very few plants, as the wall planter is only half the depth of normal containers.

2 *Formal plantings suit these containers well. Here, the centerpiece is a rather striking coleus. You may need to look through a batch of plants before finding a well-shaped specimen.*

3 *The back row is made up of bedding salvias. From a box of 15 plants, four of the same shape and size were chosen to maintain the symmetrical shape of the design.*

4 *The front row consists of four French marigolds placed in pairs on either side of the coleus. Choose the best plants and use up the rest in other containers or around the garden.*

5 *Avoid breaking up the rootballs when you plant them. If space is restricted, you may need to squeeze the roots slightly to make them fit in. This is no problem if you are careful.*

6 *Fill in the spaces between the rootballs with more soil and scatter some over the surface of the finished display. Unfurl any leaves that have been tucked in.*

Salvia 'Vanguard'

Coleus hybrid

French marigold 'Aurora Fire'

8 *The finished arrangement is likely to dry out more quickly than a container at ground level, so check it twice daily and water it as often as necessary to keep the soil moist.*

7 *As the container is relatively small but well filled, water it two or three times, allowing the water to soak in well before adding any more.*

Climbers in containers

If wall space is limited, you can grow climbers up pergola poles and pillars or over arches. And if there does not happen to be any soil there, grow the climber in a container. Another good way of growing climbers, especially if you have a small garden, is on a framework that stands in the pot itself. 'Obelisks', such as the trellis shown here, are becoming very popular. This one is available ready made, packed flat, and can be assembled in minutes at home. Some climbers make good plants for containers. Of the annual climbers, plants such as canary creeper (*Tropaeolum peregrinum*), sweet peas, cup-and-saucer vine (*Cobaea scandens*), morning glory (*Ipomoea*), and Chilean glory vine (*Eccremocarpus*) are all good choices. But if you want a climber that can be left in the same container for several years at a time, a clematis is ideal.

All climbers in pots need generous feeding. Start two weeks after planting in the container, using a liquid or soluble tomato feed. This contains potash, which encourages flowering. After a few weeks, alternate this with a general-purpose feed.

Climbers also need frequent watering, especially when the container fills with roots, as the potting mixture dries out quickly at this stage. Although most annual climbers are real sun-lovers, clematis prefer cool conditions at the roots. In a sunny spot, stand other containers around them so that their foliage shades the soil and the base of the plant. Prune clematis in containers as if they were growing in the garden; pruning strategies vary from one variety to another, so keep the instructions that come on the back of the label when you buy the plant. After three years, tip the plant carefully out of its pot in early spring before it starts growing, carefully shake off the old soil and repot the clematis back into the same tub or one that is a size larger, using fresh potting mixture.

3 Fill the tub with a soil-based potting mix, leaving 1in(2.5cm) around the rim for watering. This still allows plenty of space for the rootball to develop.

4 Plant clematis deeper than they were planted in their original pots. Then if a plant suffers from clematis wilt, which kills the shoots, new ones can regrow from below the surface.

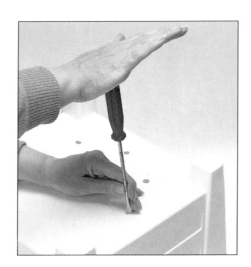

1 Plastic containers, such as this tub, have no holes in the base. Tap out the 'weak points' with a screwdriver if you want to use them outside.

2 Cover the drainage holes with 'crocks' - pieces of broken clay flowerpot - to stop the potting mix running out later on.

5 *Remove the cane that supports the plant when you buy it and separate the stems slightly. Arrange the trellis obelisk so that the legs stand firmly in the corners of the tub and press it down gently.*

6 *Space the stems evenly around the support frame and tie them loosely in place. If the plant is going to be seen mainly from one direction, make sure the plant's 'best side' faces front.*

7 *Water well in to settle the soil around the plant roots and the legs of the obelisk. If the soil sinks or the obelisk tips to one side, add more soil, adjust the obelisk and rewet the soil.*

8 *Most clematis prefer a coolish spot where the roots are in shade but the tops can grow into sunlight. Tie new growth in regularly to maintain a good shape, and remove dead flowers.*

Clematis 'Bees Jubilee'

Planting a cherry tree in a patio container

If you do not have enough room to grow fruit trees in the ground, you can keep them in large pots. Small pots measuring less than 12-14in(30-35cm) are not suitable, as they dry out quickly when full of roots; when this happens, the trees shed their fruit. Apples, pears and cherries growing on a semi-dwarfing rootstock (e.g. Colt) are the most suitable for growing in pots, and figs are superb, as their roots need to be restricted to encourage the plants to crop well. Choose self-fertile varieties of fruit tree unless you are certain that there are suitable pollinators (other trees of the same type but different varieties that flower at the same time) growing nearby, otherwise you will not get a crop. Cherry 'Stella' (shown here), apple 'Greensleeves' and 'Conference' pear all produce a crop when grown on their own. Alternatively, grow a family tree. This is a single tree with several different varieties grafted onto it. Each branch produces a different variety of apple or pear (not both on the same tree), which are chosen to cross-pollinate each other.

Pot-grown apples and pears can be trained as half-standards, bush trees or cordons. Train cherries and figs as standard trees, bushes or fans. Every three years, take the fruit trees out of their pots while they are dormant in early spring and shake most of the old soil from the roots. Trim off 10 percent of the old roots, then repot the plants into fresh potting mixture, either back into the same pot or into a container one size larger.

4 *Add more soil around the roots, firming it down gently. Barely cover the surface of the rootball with fresh soil if you can see any roots showing, but do not bury it deeply.*

1 *Cover the drainage holes of a large pot with crocks. Make sure you can still move the pot once it is filled with potting mixture.*

2 *Add 2in(5cm) of soil-based potting mix. Leave room for the rootball plus a gap of 1in(2.5cm) at the rim for watering.*

3 *Remove the tree from its old pot. Tease out any over-crowded roots. Sit the tree in the center of the new container. Push the canes in around the edge of the pot.*

Prune cherries in spring and summer, not in winter.

In summer, cut back overgrown main shoots to a weak side shoot to reshape the tree.

5 *Water the plant well in. A clay pot will dry out faster than a plastic one, so check daily. Do not allow the soil to dry out.*

In spring, cut out any shoots that are growing where you do not want them and tie the rest to the canes. The closer to the horizontal, the heavier the crop will be.

6 *This tree has been trained into a fan shape. To keep the shape, tie the new shoots up to the supporting framework or they will grow out to the front.*

7 *Being flat, a fan-trained fruit tree takes up less room than a normal tree. Stand the pot against a wall or tie the tree to a trellis or fence. The shelter they provide leads to earlier ripening fruit, and makes the crop easier to protect from birds.*

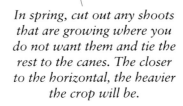

177

A classic strawberry pot

Strawberries are both ornamental and productive in containers. If you do not have room for a conventional strawberry bed, a planter such as this is ideal, as you can pack plenty of plants into a very small space. For early strawberries, move the planter into a cold or slightly heated greenhouse in midwinter and the fruit will be ready to pick several weeks earlier than usual. Strawberry plants can be bought cheaply as young 'runners' in the fall or as pot-grown plants in the fall and spring. Continue planting even when the plants are in flower, but do not allow the roots to dry out. Most strawberries look pretty when flowering, but now you can obtain varieties with pink flowers instead of white ones. Some of these are intended to be mainly ornamental, with small strawberries as a bonus, but others give a good crop of fruit as well. Keep them well watered and feed every week with liquid tomato feed, from flowering time until after the crop has been picked.

Hold the rootball under the planting pocket and gently push the leafy top of the plant out through the hole.

3 Knock the plants out of their pots. The rootballs of pot-grown strawberries will be too big to fit into the planting pockets of the pot, so plant them from the inside. Secure the plants by firming the potting mix around the roots.

1 This pot has a very large drainage hole in the base, so instead of using a single crock, it is better to heap a small handful of crocks over it. These will help to keep the soil in the pot.

2 Fill the pot to 1in(2.5cm) below the bottom row of planting pockets in the side, using a soil-based potting mixture, which is heavy enough to keep the pot stable.

4 As you complete each layer of plants, top the container up with more potting mixture to just below the base of the next row of planting pockets until you reach the rim of the pot. Firm the soil gently down around the plant roots.

5 Depending on the size of the container, plant two or three strawberry plants in the top of the pot so that it is well filled. Use a little more potting mixture to fill any gaps between the plants.

6 Water the plants thoroughly and very slowly, so that the moisture soaks in and does not run out through the planting holes.

'Serenata' has pink flowers and a useful crop of fruit.

7 Position the completed planter in a sheltered, sunny spot and feed and water it regularly. Replace the potting mix and the plants every two or three years to keep the container productive.

Trim off the runners to encourage the parent plants to fruit.

179

Planting a trough of culinary herbs

1 *Choose a terracotta trough measuring about 7x16in(18x40cm). Cover the drainage holes in the bottom with curved pieces of clean, broken clay pot, known as 'crocks'.*

Culinary herbs are always useful in the kitchen, but there is no reason why they should not look good in the garden, too. A trough of fresh herbs makes a most attractive feature by the kitchen door, where it is handy for picking. Herbs need a sheltered sunny spot to do well, so if your back door is not in the sun (or you use a lot of herbs) try having two troughs - one by the back door and the other where growing conditions are better - and switch them over regularly. When choosing herbs to plant, choose those you use most in cooking. Some of the best include those shown here, namely parsley, chives, rosemary, dill, sage and thyme. Colored-leaved varieties of popular herbs, such as tricolor and purple sage and variegated thyme, look better but taste just as good as the plain green ones. You could also add an unusual herb, such as the silver-leaved curry plant shown here. It looks attractive and really does smell and taste faintly of curry - try it in salads. Herbs are easy to care for. In a trough, they need regular feeding; you can use any good liquid feed, but those that contain seaweed improve flavor. Avoid overwatering. Herbs are fairly drought-resistant and would rather be slightly on the dry side than too wet.

2 *Cover the crocks with 1in(2.5cm) of grit. This allows surplus water to seep out of the drainage holes, but stops the potting mix washing out.*

Choose contrasting plants to put in next to each other. This is dill, which has feathery foliage that tastes faintly of aniseed.

3 *Fill the trough to within 2in(5cm) of the rim with good-quality soil-based potting mixture. Leave it loose and fluffy - do not firm it down.*

4 *Arrange the plants, still in their pots, in the trough. Put contrasting leaf colors, shapes and textures next to each other. Move the plants around until you like the effect.*

5 *Lift all the plants out of the trough and then gently knock each one out of its pot ready for planting. If the plant does not slide out easily, give the pot a sharp tap on a hard surface to loosen it.*

Thyme 'Silver Posie' is compact, variegated and edible. Use it in the same way as the normal plain green thyme.

Terracotta is porous, so plants dry out quickly - ideal for herbs, which dislike damp.

6 *It is easiest to start planting from one end of the trough, as each plant holds the next in place. Stagger the position of alternate plants.*

7 *If the herbs came in round pots, there will be gaps between the rootballs where they do not quite fit together. Fill these spaces with a few extra handfuls of potting mixture.*

8 *Stand the completed trough in a sunny, sheltered spot and support it on pot 'feet' so that surplus water can run away easily. Water it thoroughly to settle the plants in.*

Dill

Tricolor sage

Rosemary

Purple sage

Curry plant

Parsley

Chives

Thyme 'Silver Posie'

Setting up a vegetable garden in containers

When there is no room for a vegetable plot, why not grow a selection of vegetables and salads in containers? Some kinds are very decorative when grown in this way. Good choices include tomatoes, peppers, eggplants, cucumbers, climbing and dwarf beans, edible podded peas and lettuce, all of which are productive and pretty.

Choose outdoor varieties of tomato that ripen well, even in cooler conditions. Modern varieties of outdoor cucumber look and taste like the greenhouse types (which do not do well out of doors). Vegetables that are normally grown in glasshouses, such as peppers and eggplants, need a very warm, sunny, sheltered spot to do well, though any edibles in containers need sun for at least half the day. Plant into a good soil-based mixture, and keep crops well watered and regularly fed. If the soil is allowed to dry out, the crops tend to develop problems. Lettuce may bolt; runner beans fail to set, and tomatoes can develop unsightly circles of black tissue at the end furthest from the stalk. As for feeding, this should begin one to two weeks after planting. Apply liquid or soluble feeds at least once a week from then on, but follow the manufacturer's directions. Give tomatoes, peppers and eggplants diluted tomato feed. Leafy crops and beans do best on a general-purpose feed.

3 Plant crops that grow in rows, such as lettuce, in a trough. Choose large individual pots for 'specimen' crops, such as tomatoes.

1 Choose large clay or plastic containers in a range of shapes and sizes to create an interesting, varied, edible plant arrangement.

2 Fill the containers to within 1in (2.5cm) of the rim with good-quality soil-based potting mix. They will be heavy once filled; stand them in their final position before beginning.

5 Plant runner beans around the edge of a wide container; if you have a few plants left over, plant them in a circle in the middle of the tub. Choose healthy, undamaged plants.

Outdoor tomato 'Alicante'

4 You put the plants more closely together than if they were in the garden as they are growing in richer soil - it is, in fact, potting mix - and they will be receiving more intensive care.

Space runner beans 6-8in (15-20cm) apart.

Space 'Little Gem' lettuces 6in(15cm) apart.

Index to Plants

Credits

The majority of the photographs featured in this book have been taken by Neil Sutherland and are © Colour Library Books. The publishers wish to thank the following photographers for providing additional photographs, credited here by page number and position on the page, i.e. (B)Bottom, (T)Top, (C)Center, (BL)Bottom left, etc.

Gillian Beckett: 112(BR), 113(TC)
Eric Crichton: 52, 54(BL), 59(TR, BR), 74(BL,R), 75(B), 95(CR), 96(TR), 100(TR), 101(B), 126(L,BR), 127(TL), 129(BL)
John Feltwell/Garden Matters: 65(TL,R)
R. & C. Foord: 119(TC)
John Glover: 14, 27(TR,BR), 53, 55(R), 54-55(C), 63(BL,TR,BR), 75(TL,TR), 85(BL), 106(BR), 136, 161(C), 163(BL)
S. & O. Mathews: 109(BR)
Natural Image/Bob Gibbons: 116(T), 118
Clive Nichols: 15, 92 (Exbury Gardens, Hampshire), 94(T)
Harry Smith Photographic Collection: 161(B)
Elizabeth Whiting Associates: 98-99(TC)

Acknowledgments

The publishers would like to thank the following for providing plants and photographic facilities: Bridgemere Garden World, near Nantwich in Cheshire, particularly John Ravenscroft and Rosalind Harrington; Russell's Garden Center, near Chichester, Sussex; Stapeley Water Gardens, near Nantwich in Cheshire, particularly Maria Farmer, Chris Adams, Kim Clarkson, Kevin Walley, Ron Hampson, Barry Sharps and Sarah Davies. Thanks are also due to Country Gardens Alfold, near Cranleigh, Surrey for providing plants and containers for photography and to Simon Chapman (Prototype Communications) and Hozelock for supplying pumps and other aquatic equipment for photography. The following companies provided liner and underlay samples for photography: Midland Butyl Liners, Bradshaws, Glass Art Pools, Hozelock. The garden models were prepared by June Carter and Stuart Watkinson of Ideas into Print. A number of garden design features have been photographed at the RHS Chelsea Flower Shows of 1987-1993. The publishers would like to acknowledge the following garden owners and designers: Mrs. Jones, Mr. Selwyn-Smith, Mrs. H. Kenison, and F. & G. Whiten.